25 YEARS OF RECORD HOUSES

25 YEARS OF

RECORD HOUSES

Edited by Herbert L. Smith, Jr., AIA

Architectural Record Books

MCGRAW-HILL BOOK COMPANY

New York
St. Louis
San Francisco
Auckland
Bogotá
Hamburg
Johannesburg
London
Madrid
Mexico
Montreal
New Delhi
Panama
Paris
São Paulo
Singapore
Sydney
Tokyo
Toronto

ARCHITECTURAL RECORD BOOKS

Affordable Houses Designed by Architects
Apartments, Townhouses and Condominiums, 3/e
The Architectural Record Book of Vacation Houses, 2/e
Architecture 1970–1980: A Decade of Change
Buildings for Commerce and Industry
Buildings for the Arts
Contextual Architecture: Responding to Existing Style
Energy-Efficient Buildings
Engineering for Architecture
Great Houses for View Sites, Beach Sites, Sites in the Woods,
    Meadow Sites, Small Sites, Sloping Sites, Steep Sites, and Flat Sites
Hospitals and Health Care Facilities
Houses Architects Design for Themselves
Houses of the West
Institutional Buildings: Architecture of the Controlled Environment
Interior Spaces Designed by Architects, 2/e
Places for People: Hotels, Motels, Restaurants, Bars, Clubs,
    Community Recreation Facilities, Camps, Parks, Plazas, Playgrounds
Public, Municipal and Community Buildings
Religious Buildings
Recycling Buildings: Renovations, Remodelings, Restorations, and Reuses
Techniques of Successful Practice
A Treasury of Contemporary Houses

ARCHITECTURAL RECORD SERIES BOOKS

Ayers: Specifications for Architecture, Engineering and Construction
Feldman: Building Design for Maintainability
Heery: Time, Cost and Architecture
Hopf: Designer's Guide to OSHA
Portman and Barnett: The Architect as Developer
Redstone: The New Downtowns

The editors for this book were Patricia Markert and Joan Zseleczky.
The production supervisors were Carol Frances and Theresa Leaden.
The book was designed by Jan V. White.
It was set in Roma by Kingsport Press.
Printed and bound by Halliday Lithograph Corporation.

1234567890 HDHD 890987654321

ISBN 0-07-002357-3

Library of Congress Cataloging in Publication Data

Main entry under title:

Twenty-five years of record houses.

   1.   Architecture, Domestic—United States.
2.   Dwellings—United States.   3.   Architecture—
Details.   I.   Smith, Herbert L., Jr.   II.   Architectural
record.
NA7205.T84   728.3′7′0973   80–26065
ISBN 0-07-002357-3

CONTENTS

PREFACE

Recently, for a lecture on "The Contemporary American House" at the Smithsonian Institution, I was asked to trace the influence of Frank Lloyd Wright, Le Corbusier and Mies van der Rohe. I balked a bit, for, unfortunately, this limited view of the paramount influences on U.S. domestic architecture during the last quarter century is an all too pervasive one—particularly among younger architects and students, the general public and all the foreigners who continue to come to our country to study our newer houses.

Certainly, there are the strong, underlying influences of those three masters. But they are so intertwined with layers of other vigorous ideas and invention, by other superbly talented architects, that it is often difficult for any but a dedicated historian to unravel them. And I'm not an historian, but a lifelong, dedicated observer with, I trust, a fairly critical eye.

And as an observer, I can't help but note a lot of pessimism and rejection of the recent past brewing in the current, widespread architectural soul-searching.

I'm neither pessimistic nor do I reject the modern movement—especially in houses. This year marks the 25th anniversary of *Record Houses* (which I started in 1956 as the, then, only showcase completely devoted to good contemporary residential design), and to celebrate the event, I was asked to put together this book reviewing the period by choosing from among the 514 houses by 333 architects which have, so far, received *Architectural Record's* awards (see page *x*). After carefully reviewing all the houses we published in those 25 *Record Houses* issues, and painfully paring down the list to what I believe is a fairly representative selection of 57 houses, I am more convinced than ever of the continuing, nationwide vitality, ingenuity, inventiveness and talent of architects who design houses, even in face of the current drastic repercussion on home building caused by the nation's economy. For we at *Architectural Record* continue to see many extraordinarily good houses being finished even now. I'm not pessimistic because I believe that we're simply back where we recurrently are—questioning, proposing, and refining fresh (or re-discovered) ideas,—and experimenting.

Because of all this, the houses in this book are not presented chronologically, but divided into six chapters reflecting some major contributions and thematic developments in contemporary house design that—I am convinced—are valid whether one is a traditionalist, post-modernist, or only interested in "marketability." The arrangement of houses into the various chapters has been purely to emphasize the topics—all of the houses are very sensitively planned and designed for their clients, and each might have been included in any chapter. Each section is accompanied by the gently critical humor of cartoons by the late Alan Dunn, who drew most of them for the early years of *Record Houses*. A thoughtful, summary chronology through the twenty-five years—to put things in *that* perspective—is provided by Barclay Gordon, editor-in-charge of *Record Houses* since 1973, in the following introduction.

Herbert L. Smith, Jr., AIA

1,2

INTRODUCTION

Meeting in 1956 in Los Angeles, AIA members took "Architecture for the Good Life" as their convention theme. But to see the good life given characteristically mid-century expression, they had only to lift their eyes to La Cresenta, a hillside district overlooking the city, where Richard Neutra had recently completed the Serulnic house (**1,2**). In its reduction of forms to the simplest planar elements, in its openness, its sense of withdrawal from urban life, its cantilevers, its built-ins, and its general adaptability to informal lifestyles, the Serulnic house summarized, as well as any single house could, the collective vision of the good life, a vision that many middle-class but upwardly mobile Americans had carried out of the postwar.

Other excellent designs from that first issue of RECORD HOUSES sounded similar themes. Most were single story, family-oriented, direct, and were sheltered by roofs that were flat or sloped almost imperceptibly. And like the Graves house (**3**) by Cecil Elliott, most got a lot of mileage out of post and beam. To detail the large window walls that were the pride and joy of many, architects relied on Mondrianesque patterns of mullion and muntin in endless variations. In subse-

3

6,7

10,11

4

quent issues there were courtyard houses by Eliot Noyes (**4**) and Marcel Breuer (**5**). These were houses that rested behind flinty field-stone walls, designs that promised seclusion, repose, and infinite heart's ease. There were two houses by Ulrich Franzen with bold, diamond truss roofs built over graceful podiums. And there were houses by other architects that bristled with grilles or articulated sun screens.

What is important about these houses, beyond their formalism, is their level of innovation. Their architects shared a belief in the idea of progress through greater efficiency and comfort. Ideas like the pass-through, open planning, freestanding fireplaces, heat pumps, conversation pits, integrated kitchens and compartmentalized baths all passed quickly into general usage and then into the stock-and-trade banalities of developer housing. Readers who do not remember the '50s, or who (thanks to shows like *Grease* or *Happy Days*) think of the '50s only as pedal pushers, jalopies, stereos and Saturday night wrestling should look at these houses again. As a group they are still wonderfully appealing, and the best of them have lost none of their persuasiveness.

The recession of 1957-58 was no more than a brief interruption in the home-building public's pursuit of the good life, but as surely as it swept away the Edsel, it marked a point of deflection in housing design. The freshest, most interesting houses of the early '60s began to have a different feel. Harry Weese's house in Barrington, Illinois (**6, 7**) signaled changes to come. In the general playfulness of its forms, its use of interior ladders and flying bridges, in its decidedly personal character, the Weese house anticipated an important shift in emphasis. To the idea of progress through convenience and comfort that had preoccupied the residential designers of the '50s—and which architects and their clients were now starting to take for granted—a new requirement was added: the liberation of building forms.

This "new freedom," as it was often called, showed first in roof design. It led to exuberant concrete or plywood vaults and sometimes to hyperbolic paraboloids. In 1961 it led Jules Gregory to the double conoid roofs of his own New Jersey residence (**8**), and Robert Browne to the two-legged sculptural columns and 72-foot-long folded plates of the Vereen house on Biscayne Bay (**9**). But

long-span techniques, however arresting, however seductive, had limited application in residential design. Architects knew it, enjoyed it while it lasted, then quickly went in other directions.

Paul Rudolph, a masterful form-giver and never one to do things by halves, produced the eye-popping Milam house (**10, 11**) in 1963. Its cubistic forms did not depend on long-span, but generated enormous sculptural interest using the simplest of materials: flat slab and concrete block. Its interiors were a study in the subtle but vigorous manipulation of space. Tasso Katselas' own house (**12, 13**), completed in 1964, spoke eloquently of masonry's richness and variety, but "a space worth living in" was his first design imperative, and he achieved it with something to spare.

The exquisite articulation of its parts (the roof is "floated"), the intense complication of its forms, and the brilliant modulation of its spaces all mark Ralph Rapson's 1966 Pillsbury house (**14, 15**) as a summation of much of what this period was about. Looking out from five linked pavilions across a Minnesota prairie as vast as it was bountiful, the Pillsbury house was practically a metaphor for fulfill-

5

8

12,13

9

14,15

17

19

ment. It brought to a climax one line residential development, a line that might have gone further had the national mood not drifted so inexorably toward protest.

Not since the '20s had architects enjoyed such freedom, and at no time in the past had American life been so affluent or full of possibilities. The houses of the middle and early '60s exulted in these possibilities and explored them in all their fullness.

Out of the protest movement, out of the savage inner-city riots, the marches, the sit-ins, the bitter experience in Vietnam, and out of the counter-cultural alternatives, such as they were, a reluctant and somewhat uncomfortable reappraisal was almost certain to come. Architects were not exempt. Their dialogue was sometimes factious. Some turned to the inner-city with a heightened sense of social purpose; some dismissed the private house as "elitist" and no longer "relevant." The difficulty was that Americans, in spite of rising land and building costs, wanted houses as much as ever, and were apparently willing to make whatever sacrifices were necessary to satisfy this need. No design consensus was possible, or perhaps even desireable. One form that emerged (or reemerged)

somewhat incongruously was the white box. The Smith house (**16**) by Richard Meier in 1968 and those that came after it were abstract, purist, reductionist, and—in Meier's hands at least—maddeningly beautiful. Others adopted the form with less success. But interest in the white box did not extend much beyond the Northeast. Elsewhere architects were looking for—and finding—more relaxed, modest, vernacular idioms that wore well and had a touch of regionalism in their massing and finishes. In its prickly weathered shakes and saltbox shape, Norman Jaffe's 1971 Perlbinder house (**17**) did just that. With some feeling of self-deprecation, so did the Binker barn (**18**) by Moore and Turnbull a continent away.

To the search for an expression or range of expressions compatible with the '70s, the Arab oil embargo of 1973 lent a peculiar urgency. Those who read it as a foretaste of things to come acted promptly to make their designs more energy efficient. Some went directly to active solar systems. A few, like Don Metz in New Hampshire (**19**) and Florida architect William Morgan, found renewed interest in earth-sheltered houses. For most, though, it was a matter of thickening walls,

readjusting fenestration, tightening details, and looking with greater sensitivity at the sites on which they built. Blake Millar's heavy timber house (**20**), with its louvers, insulated shutters, and finely-tuned mechanical systems, reflects these new priorities.

As the new decade began, it was clear that a beginning had been made, but much more would be required if our options as a profession—indeed as a nation—are not to be foreclosed.

Even the quickest look backward over the twenty-five years just ended reminds us that residential design has been strikingly rich and diverse. Because it is a field where the penalty for failure is relatively small, it is a field where innovation flourishes. And because it is a field that affects our daily lives so directly and so personally, it tells us a great deal about ourselves; occasionally—like a highly polished mirror—a little more than we wanted to know. It continues to reflect our hopes and fancies. Now, at another time of uncertainty and shifting emphasis, at a time when the good life will almost certainly mean doing more with less, the image it throws back at us in RECORD HOUSES and elsewhere will be especially telling. —*Barclay F. Gordon*

16

18

20

THE AWARD-WINNING ARCHITECTS OF 25 YEARS OF RECORD HOUSES

ABBOTT, CARL
1972: Sarasota, FL
ABBOTT, RICHARD OWEN
1969: Westbrook, CT
AECK ASSOCIATES
1958: Callaway Gardens, GA
AMES, ANTHONY
1978: Atlanta, GA
ANDERSON, BARBARA & ALLAN
1972: Rye, NY
ANDRUS, MOULTON
1978: Park County, WY
ANSHEN & ALLEN
1956: San Rafael, CA
1960: Sunnyvale, CA
ARANGO, JORGE
1970: Miami, FL
THE ARCHITECTS COLLABORATIVE
1957: Bedford, MA
1959: Provincetown, MA
1961: Norton, MA
ARCHITECTS DESIGN GROUP
1971: Harrison, NY
ARCHITECTURAL RESOURCES CAMBRIDGE
1972: Lincoln, MA
ARLEY RINEHART ASSOCIATES
1976: Perry Park, CO
ASTLE, NEIL & ASSOCIATES
1972: Wausa, NE
1977: Nebraska
AYDELOTT, A. L. & ASSOCIATES
1959: Helena, AK
BAHR HANNA VERMEER & HAECKER
1975: Fremont, NE
BAKER & BLAKE
1971: Annandale-on-Hudson, NY
BAKER ROTHSCHILD HORN BLYTH
1979: Philadelphia, PA
BARINGER, RICHARD E.
1958: Highland Park, IL
BARNES, EDWARD LARRABEE
1957: Mount Kisco, NY
1959: Chappaqua, NY
1967: Connecticut
1968: New York State
1976: Mt. Desert Island, ME
BARNSTONE, HOWARD
1973: Galveston, TX
BARNSTONE, HOWARD & EUGENE AUBRY
1965: Houston, TX
BARRON, ERROL
1980: New Orleans, LA
BASSETTI & MORSE
1962: Mercer Island, WA
BEADLE, ALFRED N.
1965: Phoenix, AZ
BECKER, ROBERT
1980: Mercer Island, WA
BECKETT, WILLIAM S.
1956: Beverly Hills, CA
BEHN & GAVIN
1973: Santa Cruz County, CA
BEHN, PETER
1979: Berkeley, CA
BENNETT & TUNE
1970: Lexington, KY
BERKES, WILLIAM J.
1964: Wayland, MA
BETTS, HOBART
1970: Londonderry, VT
1974: West Hampton, NY
1975: Englewood, NJ
1976: Vermont
1977: Long Island, NY
1979: Quogue, Long Island, NY
BINKLEY ASSOCIATES
1964: Glencoe, IL
BIRKERTS, GUNNAR & ASSOCIATES
1968: Grand Rapids, MI
BIRKERTS, GUNNAR & FRANK STRAUB
1961: Northville, MI
BISSELL & WELLS
1979: Nantucket Island, MA
BLISS & CAMPBELL
1963: Minnesota
1964: Minneapolis, MN
BLOODGOOD, JOHN D.
1969: Des Moines, IA
BLUM, VAPORCIYAN & MITCH
1972: Franklin, MI
BOHLIN & POWELL
1976: West Cornwall, CT

BOLTON & BARNSTONE
1956: Houston, TX
1957: Houston, TX
1959: Houston, TX
BOLTON, P. M. & ASSOCIATES
1963: Houston, TX
BOOTH, LAURENCE
1980: Evanston, IL
BOOTH & NAGLE
1970: Chicago, IL
1972: Minnesota
1974: Des Moines, IA
1975: Vashon Island, WA
1976: Hinsdale, IL
BOOTH NAGLE & HARTRAY
1978: Glencoe, IL
BREUER, MARCEL & ASSOCIATES
1956: Andover, MA
1958: Duluth, MN
1960: Andover, MA
1961: Baltimore, MD
1978: South Orange, NJ
1979: Big Sur, CA
BREUER, MARCEL & HERBERT BECKHARD
1967: Litchfield, CT
BROWN, WALTER/LAWRENCE JACOBS
1977: Westchester, NY
BROWNE, ROBERT B.
1958: Key Biscayne, FL
1961: Miami, FL
1962: Key Vaca, FL
BROWNE, ROBERT B. & RUFUS NIMS
1960: Miami Beach, FL
BROWNSON, JACQUES C.
1956: Geneva, IL
BRUCK, F. FREDERICK
1965: Cambridge, MA
BRUDER, WILLIAM
1977: Arizona
BUFF, STRAUB & HENSMAN
1961: Los Angeles, CA
BULL FIELD VOLKMANN STOCKWELL
1972: San Francisco, CA
1978: Napa Valley, CA
BULL, HENRIK
1964: El Dorado Hills, CA
BUNSHAFT, GORDON
1966: East Hampton, NY
BURGER & COPLANS
1973: San Francisco, CA
BURK, LEBRETON & LAMANTIA
1958: Lake Charles, LA
BURLEY, ROBERT ASSOCIATES
1973: Maine
BYSTROM, ARNE
1980: Whidbey Island, WA
CALDWELL, JAMES E., JR.
1975: Woodside, CA
CALLENDER, JOHN HANCOCK
1957: Darien, CT
CALLISTER, PAYNE & BISCHOFF
1976: Belvedere, CA
CAMPBELL & WONG & ASSOCIATES
1964: Colusa, CA
CANNADY, WILLIAM T.
1973: Houston, TX
CARDWELL, RICHARD
1977: Puget Sound, WA
CARVER, NORMAN F., JR.
1960: Kalamazoo, MI
1961: Kalamazoo, MI
1962: Kalamazoo, MI
CHAFEE, JUDITH
1970: Connecticut
1975: Tucson, AZ
1979: Arizona
CHAPELL, DON
1977: East Hampton, NY
CHENG, JAMES
1977: Vancouver, BC
CHIMACOFF/PETERSON
1973: Montauk, NY
1976: Morristown, NJ
COLBERT, CHARLES
1965: New Orleans, LA
COMBS, EARL B.
1971: Fire Island, NY
CONKLIN, WILLIAM J.
1959: Peeksville, NY
COPLAND, HAGMAN, YAW
1980: Aspen, CO
CORBETT, MARIO
1957: Healdsburg, CA

COSTON, TRUETT H.
1954: Oklahoma City, OK
CRISSMAN & SOLOMON
1977: New York State
1979: New Vernon, NJ
CRITES & McCONNELL
1973: Burlington, IA
CUETARA, EDWARD
1974: Martha's Vineyard, MA
CURTIS & DAVIS
1956: Pascagoula, MS
1957: New Orleans, LA
1959: New Orleans, LA
1960: New Orleans, LA
1964: New Orleans, LA
DALAND, ANDREW
1970: Lake George, NY
DAMORA, ROBERT
1962: Cape Cod, MA
DARROW, LEE STUART
1960: Mill Valley, CA
DART, EDWARD D.
1963: Highland Park, IL
1966: Lake Forest, IL
DAVIS, BRODY & ASSOCIATES
1972: Westport, CT
DAVIS, BRODY & WISNIEWSKI
1957: Huntington Valley, PA
1959: Peeksville, NY
DAVIS, MARY LUND
1964: Tacoma, WA
DESIGN CONSORTIUM
1978: St. Paul, MN
DESIGNERS & BUILDERS
1957: Greenwich, CT
DESMOND, JOHN
1960: Hammond, LA
DeVIDO, ALFRED
1969: East Hampton, NY
1972: Westchester County, NY
1975: Long Island, NY
1976: Long Island, NY
1978: Watermill, NY
DORMAN, RICHARD L. & ASSOCIATES
1959: Encino, CA
1967: Sherman Oaks, CA
EDWARDS & PORTMAN
1965: Atlanta, GA
ELLIOT, CECIL D.
1956: Mt. Airy, NC
ELLWOOD, CRAIG
1959: Malibu, CA
1964: West Los Angeles, CA
ELTING, WINSTON
1965: Ligonier, PA
ENGLEBRECHT, ROBERT MARTIN
1966: San Rafael, CA
ERICKSON, ARTHUR/ARCHITECTS
1975: Vancouver, BC
ERICKSON/MASSEY
1969: Cotuit, MA
ERNEST, ROBERT
1962: Atlantic Beach, FL
FAULKNER, AVERY C.
1966: McLean, VA
FIELD, JOHN L.
1961: Los Altos Hills, CA
FISHER-FRIEDMAN ASSOCIATES
1965: Millbrae, CA
1966: Belvedere, CA
1972: Belvedere, CA
FISHER, NES, CAMPBELL & PARTNERS
1966: Baltimore, MD
1969: Owing Mills, MD
FITZPATRICK, KIRBY WARD
1976: St. Helena, CA
FITZPATRICK, ROBERT E.
1969: Yorktown, NY
FLANSBURGH, EARL R. & ASSOCIATES
1965: Weston, MA
1966: Dover, MA
1967: Harvard, MA
1968: Weston, MA
1973: Lincoln, MA
1975: Cape Cod, MA
FLETCHER, WILLIAM
1958: Portland, OR
FOOTE, STEVEN
1980: Connecticut
FRANZEN, ULRICH
1956: Rye, NY
1958: Rye, NY
1959: Rye, NY
1960: Essex, CT

1962: New London, CT
1963: Greenwich, CT
1964: Westport, CT
1966: New Canaan, CT
1967: Long Island Sound, NY
1968: Long Island, NY
1979: Bridgehampton, NY
GELARDIN BRUNER COTT
1977: Massachusetts
GEORGE, F. MALCOLM
1968: Berkeley, CA
GIBBS, HUGH & DONALD GIBBS
1970: Palos Verdes Penninsula, CA
GILCHRIST, JOHN ROBERT
1963: Lakewood, NJ
GILL, CRATTAN
1980: Cape Cod, MA
GLASS, FRANK B.
1964: Des Moines, IA
GLUCK, PETER L.
1973: Westminster, VT
GOETZ & HANSEN
1959: Lafayette, CA
GOLDFINGER, MYRON
1971: Waccabuc, NY
1974: New York State
1978: Chappaquiddick Island, MA
GONZALES, BENNIE M.
1967: Paradise Valley, AZ
GOODMAN, CHARLES M. ASSOCIATES
1956: Lake Barcroft, VA
GOUBERT, DELNOCE WHITNEY
1967: Morris Township, NJ
GREGORY, JULES
1961: Lambertville, NJ
1963: Verona, NJ
1966: New Jersey
GRIDER & LA MARCHE
1959: Boise, ID
GRIFFITH, NEWTON E.
1962: Edina, MN
GROSSMAN, THEODORE A., JR.
1971: Parker, CO
GROWALD, MARTIN
1971: New York State
GRUBER, MORTON M.
1969: Atlanta, GA
GUERON, HENRI CHARLES
1972: East Hampton, NY
GUND, GRAHAM
1979: Massachusetts
GUSTAVSON, DEAN L.
1960: Salt Lake City, UT
GWATHMEY & HENDERSON
1968: Purchase, NY
1969: Manchester, CT
GWATHMEY HENDERSON SIEGEL
1970: Orleans, MA
GWATHMEY SIEGEL
1973: East Hampton, NY
1975: Eastern Long Island, NY
1979: Amagansett, NY
HAID, DAVID
1968: Lakeside, MI
1971: Evanston, IL
HAMPTON, MARK
1960: Savannah, GA
1964: Tampa, FL
1968: Tampa, FL
HEIMSATH, CLOVIS B.
1966: Nassau Bay, TX
HELLMUTH, OBATA & KASSABAUM
1959: St. Louis, MO
1961: Ladue, MO
HENDERSON, RICHARD
1972: Huntington Bay, NY
HESTER-JONES & ASSOCIATES
1963: Del Mar, CA
HIRSHEN & VAN DER RYN
1969: Point Reyes, CA
HISAKA, DON & ASSOCIATES
1976: Ohio
HISS, PHILIP
1958: Sarasota, FL
HOBBS FUKUI ASSOCIATES
1978: Seattle, WA
HOLMES, D. E.
1972: Tampa, FL
HUNTER, E. H. & M. K.
1956: Manchester, NH
1960: Hanover, NH
HUYGENS & TAPPÉ
1972: Barrington, RI
1974: Darien, CT
1980: New England Coast
ILMANEN, WILLIAM J.
1968: Baltimore, MD
JACOBS, DONALD
1978: Sea Ranch, CA
JACOBSEN, HUGH NEWELL
1964: Bethesda, MD
1965: Riva, MD
1966: Martha's Vineyard, MA
1967: Washington, DC
1968: Bristol, RI
1969: Washington, DC
1970: Montgomery County, MD
1971: Easton, MD
1973: Salisbury, CT
1975: Philadelphia, PA
1976: Frederick, MD
1977: Chevy Chase, MD
1978: Washington, DC
1979: Wayzata, MN
1980: Pennsylvania

JACOBSON, PHILIP
1975: Seattle, WA
JAFFE, NORMAN
1964: Lake Mahopac, NY
1971: Sagaponack, NY
1977: Long Island, NY
1978: Old Westbury, NY
JENNEWEIN, G. P. & J. J.
1963: New York City
JOHANSEN-BHAVNANI
1978: Connecticut
JOHANSEN, JOHN MacL.
1956: New York City
1958: Connecticut
1976: Connecticut
JOHNSON, PHILIP
1957: Irvington-on-Hudson, NY
1962: Long Island, NY
JOHNSON, ROY SIGVARD
1961: Hastings-on-Hudson, NY
JONES, A. QUINCY &
FREDERICK E. EMMONS
1956: Pacific Palisades, CA
1957: San Mateo, CA
JONES, E. FAY
1978: Arkansas
JONES, WALK C., JR.
1953: Memphis, TN
JONES, WALK + FRANCIS MAH
1969: Memphis, TN
1971: Memphis, TN
KAPLAN, RICHARD D.
1970: Montauk Point, NY
KATSELAS, TASSO
1964: Pittsburgh, PA
1974: Pittsburgh, PA
KECK, GEORGE FRED—WILLIAM KECK
1958: Olympia Fields, IL
1962: Pleasant Valley, PA
1963: Highland Park, IL
1966: Burlington, IA
1967: Chicago, IL
KELLY, JOHN TERENCE
1962: Elyria, OH
KESSLER, WILLIAM & ASSOCIATES
1973: L'Arbre Croche, MI
1976: Lakeport, MI
KEYES, LETHBRIDGE & CONDON
1961: Washington, DC
1966: Bethesda, MD
KILLINGSWORTH-BRADY-SMITH
1958: Long Beach, CA
1963: Long Beach, CA
KINDORF, ROBERT
1976: Plumas County, CA
KIRK, PAUL HAYDEN
1957: Seattle, WA
1961: Bellevue, WA
KIRK, WALLACE, McKINLEY &
ASSOCIATES
1970: Mercer Island, WA
KNORR & ELLIOTT
1958: Atherton, CA
1963: Tahoe Keys, CA
1974: Riverside, CA
KOCH, CARL & ASSOCIATES
1963: Yorktown Heights, NY
KRAMER & KRAMER
1956: Maplewood, NJ
1962: Teaneck, NJ
KROEGER, KEITH ASSOCIATES
1979: Westchester, NY
KROEGER, KEITH & LEONARD PERFIDO
1971: Waccabuc, NY
KRUEGER, PAUL H.
1973: Truro, MA
KUHN & DRAKE
1962: South Plainfield, NJ
LAMANTIA, JAMES R.
1969: New Orleans, LA
LAND & KELSEY
1962: South Laguna, CA
LANDSBERG, WILLIAM W.
1957: Long Island, NY
LARSON, THOMAS
1974: Roseau, MN
LAUTNER, JOHN
1971: Malibu Beach, CA
1977: Acapulco, Mexico
LAWRENCE, SAUNDERS & CALONGNE
1957: New Orleans, LA
1958: New Orleans, LA
LEE, ROGER ASSOCIATES
1962: Berkeley, CA
LEEDY, GENE
1965: Rockledge, FL
LEELA DESIGN
1979: Guilford, CT
LEWIS, GEORGE S.
1962: Westport, CT
LIEBHARDT, FREDERICK
& EUGENE WESTON III
1965: Del Mar, CA
LITTLE, ROBERT A. & ASSOCIATES
1956: Plymouth, OH
1957: Cleveland, OH
LOVETT, WENDELL H.
1969: Bellevue, WA
1972: Mercer Island, WA
1974: Crane Island, WA
LUCKENBACH, CARL
1965: Birmingham, MI
LUNDY, VICTOR
1958: Venice, FL
1959: Sarasota, FL

MACKALL, LOUIS
1976: Nantucket, MA
MALONE & HOOPER
1957: Kentfield, CA
MARQUIS & STOLLER
1970: Marin County, CA
MASSDESIGN
1979: Westford, MA
MATSUMOTO, GEORGE
1957: Raleigh, NC
1961: Roanoke Rapids, NC
1962: Sedgefield, NC
MAYERS & SCHIFF
1970: Hawley, PA
1974: Armonk, NY
1980: Long Island, NY
McCUE BOONE TOMSICK
1973: San Mateo County, CA
McKIM, PAUL W.
1968: San Diego, CA
McLEOD, JAMES
1972: Fire Island Pines, NY
MEATHE, KESSLER & ASSOCIATES
1961: Franklin Hills, MI
1965: Grosse Pointe, MI
MEIER, RICHARD
1964: Essex Falls, NJ
1968: Darien, CT
1969: East Hampton, NY
1977: Westchester, NY
MERRILL, SIMMS & ROEHRIG
1961: Honolulu, HI
MERZ, JOSEPH G. & MARY L.
1969: Brooklyn, NY
METZ, DONALD
1974: Lyme, NH
MILLAR, C. BLAKEWAY
1975: Georgian Bay, ONT
1980: Toronto, ONT
MILLS & MARTIN
1971: Dublin, NH
MILLS, WILLIS N., JR.
1967: Van Hornesville, NY
MITHUN, RIDENOUR & COCHRAN
1960: Issaquah, WA
MLTW/MOORE TURNBULL
1967: Monterey, CA
1969: Santa Cruz, CA
1970: Pajaro Dunes, CA
1973: Sea Ranch, CA
MLTW/TURNBULL ASSOCIATES
1972: Aptos, CA
MOGER, RICHARD B.
1967: Clayton, NY
1973: Southampton, NY
MOLNY, ROBIN
1975: Aspen, CO
MOORE, ARTHUR COTTON
1972: Washington, DC
1977: Arlington, VA
1980: Washington, DC
MOORE, CHARLES W.
& RICHARD C. PETERS
1962: Corral de Tierra, CA
MOORE GROVER HARPER
1978: Guilford, CT
1978: Maryland
1979: Sagaponack, NY
1980: Connecticut
MORGAN & LINDSTROM
1979: Bainbridge Island, WA
MORGAN, WILLIAM
1963: Atlantic Beach, FL
1965: Jacksonville, FL
1966: Ponte Vedra Beach, FL
1968: Atlantic Beach, FL
1974: Jacksonville, FL
1976: Florida
1977: Florida
1980: Florida
MORRIS, LANGDON
1960: Aspen, CO
MUCHOW, W. C.
1957: Denver, CO
MYERS, BARTON
1977: Toronto, ONT
NAGLE, NORMAN C.
1957: Minneapolis, MN
NELSON & CHADWICK
1958: Kalamazoo, MI
NELSON, IBSEN A., RUSSELL B. SABIN,
GORDON B. VAREY
1963: Seattle, WA
NEMENY, GEORGE
1957: Long Island, NY
1963: Long Island, NY
1967: Rye, NY
NESKI, JULIAN & BARBARA
1968: Long Island, NY
1969: Amagansett, NY
1971: Bridgehampton, NY
1972: East Hampton, NY
1973: Remsenburg, NY
1975: Ashley Falls, MA
NEUHAUS & TAYLOR
1958: Houston, TX
NEUTRA, RICHARD J.
1956: Los Angeles, CA
1961: Los Angeles, CA
NEWMAN, HERBERT S.
1965: Woodbridge, CT
NEWMAN, RICHARD & JUDITH
1975: Fire Island, NY
NICHOLS, ROBERT
1974: Austin, TX

NIMS & BROWNE
1956: Miami, FL
NIMS, RUFUS
1957: Redington, FL
NOYES, ELIOT
1956: Hobe Sound, FL
1957: New Canaan, CT
1959: Port Chester, NY
1971: Stamford, CT
1974: Greenwich, CT
OAKLAND, CLAUDE
1964: Orange, CA
1968: Sunnyvale, CA
OBATA, GYO
1967: St. Louis, MO
OLIVER, JAMES C.
1973: Portland, OR
OLSEN, DONALD
1966: Ross, CA
OPPENHEIMER, BRADY & LEHRECKE
1963: Tappan, NY
OSMON, FRED LINN
1979: Carefree, AZ
OSSIPOFF, VLADIMIR
1960: Honolulu, HI
1963: Honolulu, HI
OVERPECK, FRAZIER
1957: Santa Monica, CA
OWEN, CHRISTOPHER H. L.
1975: Westchester County, NY
1979: Long Beach Island, NJ
1980: Stockbridge, MA
PASANELLA, GIOVANNI
1969: Winhall, VT
1970: Wellfleet, MA
PEARSON & PORTER
1973: Atlanta, GA
PEI, I. M. & ASSOCIATES
1964: Washington, DC
PEKRUHN, JOHN E.
1956: Fox Chapel Borough, PA
1958: Pittsburgh, PA
PERFIDO, LEONARD P.
1976: Weston, CT
PERRY, LYMAN
1977: Pennsylvania
PORTER/KELLY
1978: Atlanta, GA
PREDOCK, ANTOINE
1977: New Mexico
PRENTICE & CHAN, OHLHAUSEN
1970: Riverside, CT
PRICE, ROBERT BILLSBROUGH
1959: Tacoma, WA
PULLIAM, MATTHEWS & ASSOCIATES
1973: Beverly Hills, CA
QUINN, RICHARD E.
1966: Denver, CO
RADER, MORTON
1975: Marin County, CA
RAPSON, RALPH
1959: St. Paul, MN
1966: Wayzata, MN
REAM, QUINN & ASSOCIATES
1968: Denver, CO
RILEY, J. ALEXANDER
1971: Inverness, CA
ROARK, DONALD R.
1966: Golden, CO
ROBBIN & RAILLA
1966: Burbank, CA
ROCKRISE, GEORGE T.
1958: Medford, OR
1960: Atherton, CA
ROLAND-MILLER
1978: Napa, CA
ROLANDO, CHARLES R. & ASSOCIATES
1980: Carlisle, MA
ROTH, HAROLD * EDWARD SAAD
1970: Cheshire, CT
ROTH & MOORE
1980: Woodbridge, CT
RUDOLPH, PAUL
1956: Auburn, AL
1956: Sarasota, FL
1959: Casey Key, FL
1960: Cambridge, MA
1962: Tampa, FL
1963: St. John's County, FL
1965: Athens, AL
1970: New York City
1976: New York State
RUPP, WILLIAM
1960: Sarasota, FL
SALERNO, JOSEPH
1974: West Redding, CT
SALZMAN, STANLEY
1964: New York State
SAUER, LOUIS
1967: Reston, VA
1971: Margate, NJ
SCHIFFER, JOSEPH J.
1965: Concord, MA
SCHLESINGER, FRANK
1961: Doylestown, PA
SCHWIKHER & ELTING
1956: Flossmoor, IL
SCOTT, J. LAWRENCE
1977: Ohio
SEIBERT, EDWARD J.
1961: Sarasota, FL
SERT, JOSEP LLUIS
1959: Cambridge, MA
SHERWOOD, MILLS & SMITH
1957: New Canaan, CT

SHORT, SAM B. & ROSS G. MURRELL
1961: Baton Rouge, LA
SINGER, DONALD
1969: Miami, FL
1971: Coconut Grove, FL
1975: Boca Raton, FL
1978: South Miami, FL
SLACK, JOHN
1979: Omaha, NE
SMALL & BOAZ
1960: Raleigh, NC
SMITH, EDGAR WILSON
1965: Portland, OR
1967: Lake Oswego, OR
SMITH, JOSEPH N.
1959: Miami, FL
SMITH & LARSON
1973: Pebble Beach, CA
SMITH, MELVIN/NOEL YAUCH
1976: Massachusetts
SMITH & WILLIAMS
1956: Pasadena, CA
SMOTRICH & PLATT
1971: Mendham, NJ
SOBEL, ROBERT
1974: Houston, TX
SOREY, THOMAS L., JR.
1968: Oklahoma City, OK
SORIANO, RAPHAEL
1956: Bel Air, CA
SPECTER, DAVID KENNETH
1971: East Hampton, NY
SPEYER, A. JAMES
1956: Highland Park, IL
STAGEBERG, JAMES EDGAR
1962: Minneapolis, MN
1964: Chesterfield, MO
1968: Edina, MN
STRAUSS, CARL A.
1960: Cincinnati, OH
STUBBINS, HUGH
1959: Rhode Island
1967: Cambridge, MA
TERNSTROM & SKINNER
1965: South Pasadena, CA
THIRY, PAUL
1956: Seattle, WA
1958: Seattle, WA
TIGERMAN, STANLEY & ASSOCIATES
1980: Lisle, IL
TROUT ARCHITECTS
1978: Ohio
TWITCHELL & MIAO
1974: New York State
VENDENSKY, DMITRI
1975: Sea Ranch, CA
VISE, HERBERT
1967: York Harbor, ME
WAGENER, HOBART D.
1967: Boulder, CO
WARNER & GRAY
1977: California
WARRINER, JOAN & KEN
1961: Sarasota, FL
WEBB, CHARD F.
1958: Phoenixville, PA
WEBBER, ELROY ASSOCIATES
1962: South Hadley, MA
WEESE, HARRY
1960: Chicago, IL
1970: Canada
WEINER GRAN ASSOCIATES
1972: Westport, CT
WEISBACH, GERALD G.
1968: Mill Valley, CA
WEST, J. & ASSOCIATES
1965: Sarasota, FL
WEXLER & HARRISON
1963: Palm Springs, CA
WHISNANT, MURRAY
1974: Charlotte, NC
WHITTON, ROBERT
1974: Boxboro, MA
WIENER, SAMUEL G. & WILLIAM B.
& ASSOCIATES
1956: Shreveport, LA
WILKES, JOSEPH A.
& WINTHROP W. FAULKNER
1968: McLean, VA
WILLIAMS, GERALD A.
1979: Seattle, WA
WILSON, MORRIS, CRAIN & ANDERSON
1969: Houston, TX
WOEHLE, FRITZ
1964: Birmingham, AL
WOERNER, PETER KURT
1976: Guilford, CT
WOLF, JOHNSON & ASSOCIATES
1970: North Carolina
WONG, BROCCHINI & ASSOCIATES
1972: Santa Cruz, CA
WOO, YOUNG
1967: Los Angeles, CA
WOOLLEN, EVANS III
1957: Indianapolis, IN
WU, KING-LUI
1966: Old Lyme, CT
1975: Killingsworth, CT
WURSTER, BERNARDI & EMMONS
1956: Marin County, CA
YAMASAKI, LEINWEBER & ASSOCIATES
1957: Detroit, MI
ZEPHYR ARCHITECTURAL PARTNERSHIP
1980: Lanikai, HI

"If you can't stand the heat, get out of the Open Plan!"

1. THE QUEST FOR SPACE

Probably the greatest real luxury and delight in houses—to our Western culture at least—is quite simply, space. Space for all the humdrum daily activities, space for the celebrations, space for solitude and—equally important—space for the ego and the eye.

But, perversely, space has burgeoned into one of our most expensive commodities. Since World War II, a variety of factors have caused all sorts of costs to continually spiral: for financing, land, materials, labor, maintenance. And we have become (*overly* it is now evident) dependent on increasingly complex and expensive mechanisms for heating, cooling, lighting, plumbing: an unequipped, protective shell—even with handsome Doric columns—will no longer do. Nor will, in most cases, the traditionally commodious house with sizeable compartments for each specific activity. New requirements have had to be adapted for more casual lifestyles—or is it vice versa?

Challenged by all this, architects have been industrious and inventive in the creation and handling of appropriate space (real and apparent) within tighter and tighter budget restrictions. In all the houses of the quarter-century highlighted in this volume, it has been a basic, underlying concern, whatever the style or size of the house. Those singled out in this chapter only indicate the myriad spatial concepts architects have so diligently explored.

At the beginning of this period there was, of course, the infinitely rich legacy of architectural history; of the more immediate Victorianisms of our grandparents—with their frolicsome nooks and crannies, adaptable double-parlors with sliding doors, relaxing verandahs, screened porches and solariums. There was also The Way of each of the modern architecture prophets: Frank Lloyd Wright with his tactile materials reaching out into terraced landscapes; Le Corbusier with his spaces of crisply contrasting geometries; Mies van der Rohe with his

sumptuous simplicities. And there was the 1930s pioneering into American spatial modernity by such durable architects as Richard Neutra in California; George Fred and William Keck in Chicago; and Buckminster Fuller with his Dymaxion house at the Chicago World's Fair of 1933, which indicated a *still* latent future with glazed spaces wire-suspended from a central mast. Dolloped around the country were the white-walled, glass-blocked, corner-windowed, streamlined spaces of post-Art Deco.

After the building hiatus of World War II, this potpourri of concepts led, most pervasively, to solving some of the space/money/maintenance problems of the then conventional but shrinking two-story box, by minimizing hallway circulation space and re-combining traditional activities into single, larger rooms: living-dining spaces, family-room–kitchens, bedroom-studies. The ultimate of this was, of course, the Mies-inspired, basementless, one-story, totally open plan. This multi-use, "universal space," however, demanded an extreme degree of either togetherness or stoic formality that few of us could cope with.

"What's cooking?"

"Close and secure all primary wall openings, slide the sunlight roof to full closure, fasten down the canvas weather screening and close all secondary ports —it's beginning to rain."

To stress even further the expanse of the open plan, there was a concurrently decreasing use of free-standing furniture and increase in exterior glass walls. Probably the apogee of this concept—and certainly the most elegant and famous—is Philip Johnson's 1950 glass pavilion in New Caanan, Connecticut (though it does have a bedroom-baffle and an enclosed bath).

But if the extreme of this planning direction was not for everyone, endless permutations and variations of it by talented architects *were*—from great individual houses to countless small homes in developments. The ideas were not all necessarily new, but they were vigorously pursued: privacy, with open plan flexibility, was gained by use of partial partitions, sliding and folding walls, room dividers and storage units, interior walls with cut-outs and windows.

Instead of just open space, an often greater sense of *continuing* space was developed by leading the eye over, around and through the containing elements (and even through fireplaces). Walls and ceilings were extended and led the eye to the outdoors. Even mirrors extended vistas at dead ends. Sometimes these continuities became so intellectualized that, in reality, they were visible only in the plans or drawings; in some of these cases, a mental nudge was given by continuing a color or material through the spaces. In others, such as the house by Gunnar Birkerts on page 32, partitions and baffles were so arranged that the interiors appeared open from one spot, and visually closed when one moved away.

Well defined (and lower cost) living spaces outdoors—terraces, screened "Florida rooms," atriums and courtyards, covered colonnades and pergolas—were designed to reach out and augment space inside for visually connected, "indoor-outdoor" living. Much greater privacy than that afforded by flexible walls—and often with the attendant creation of more indoor-outdoor spaces—was achieved by zoning houses into two, three or more connected units for various specified purposes. These included such divisions as adult/children, passive/active, noisy/quiet, public/private, and so on, which became imperative at the peak of the baby boom. Other houses were zoned by applying Lou Kahn's concept of "servant spaces" to group utilitarian areas into clearly defined and expressed banks set off from living spaces.

While all this was being designed in a more or less horizontal or plan sense, equal thought was devoted to vertical or volumetric space. The age-old device of aggrandizing a bright, major space by entering it through a darker, lower one—a trick used to great advantage by Wright—was again brought into play. It also permitted the use of clerestory windows between roof levels for views and light. Shed, butterfly and pitched roofs were re-introduced with ceilings following the rooflines for added height. (The pitched ones were soon popularly dubbed "cathedral ceilings"!) And then followed experiments with vaults, domes (usually clear plastic), and all sorts of zig-zag or folded plate and curved or wavy roof variants—each adding its own type of vertical space. Sometimes, a single, expansive roof was used to cover a variety of indoor and outdoor spaces beneath.

Nor was the floor plane ignored. Conversation pits were set into floor slabs to remove the bulkiness of seating from direct view, and to give the occupants an illusion of much greater space above them. Split level schemes were developed to link lower heights of lesser spaces to the high ones of major rooms. Which led in due course to multi-levels ad infinitum, with Paul Rudolph's houses in the vanguard: level changes were used to define "rooms"; to heighten or reduce emphasis on various areas; to create balconies and catwalks inside and out; and, above all, to lead and tease the eye up through an increasingly complex interplay of soaring volumes. The levels also formed another effective, if athletic, way to zone a house. All this was sometimes achieved in houses of relatively small size. And in compact town- or row-houses, it brought a totally unexpected sense of space, along with some of the fun of Victorian eyries.

Color, either applied or inherent in the materials, played its constant part in visually manipulating space. Usually wrapped in overall neutral tones (or white) for unity, various areas often used color contrasts to lead the eye, to lower or heighten, widen or narrow. Artificial and day-lighting were used for similar ends. Few means for spatial effect were left unexplored.

Thus, the threshold of the 1980s finds the architectural spatial vocabulary vastly enriched, and offering an almost bewildering array of choices to help tailor a house to its occupants' needs and purse. But architecture is not a self-satisfied profession: the studying, searching, inventing goes on.

Richard J. Neutra
Los Angeles, California
1956

The decision of knowing exactly what one wants in a house is often half the battle of achieving it. Mr. and Mrs. George Serulnic were quite definite in their ideas—a spacious contemporary hillside house with a really dramatic view—but their budget was very limited. Undaunted, they bought a seemingly impossible patch of hillside that had the view, and commissioned Richard J. Neutra, an architect well known for creating the kind of house they liked, to study their problem.

By extremely careful planning and budgeting, a house was created that completely delighted the clients. Fitted on a tiny site created out of the hillside, the small house is clean-cut, good looking—and seems enormous. Open, multipurpose areas, glass walls to capitalize on the view, and simple structure and materials all add to this effect. There are even rather luxurious surprises: entrance court, bath with patio.

The house lies among scattered mountainside dwellings in La Cresenta, overlooking the Los Angeles area. There is a wonderful mountain panorama. During the day, different colored mountain slopes stretch as far as the eye can see; at night, lights of the city glitter far below. On clear days, the ocean is visible. Other houses dotting the slopes are some distance away.

The architect states that when he visited the site for the first time, there seemed no possible

The plan of the Serulnic house is handled to give good area division, utmost sense of space. The entire glass wall slides open to add terrace to living area. The sitting nook at right in photo below left converts for dining. Entrance court (below center) has reflecting pool, lush plants.

way to get up—what he saw was simply several acres of precipitous slope. A small flat site for the house was cut out of the hillside, with a long winding road built to reach it.

At the top of the winding drive, one reaches the parking area and carport. From there, one enters the house along the edge of the cut-out hillside through a small court with a shallow reflecting pool. On opening the door, one is faced with the wonderful panorama.

The open living area is bisected by a fireplace dividing the space into a family-guest room and the living room proper. A dining bay, near the kitchen, has a low table, patented by the architect, that can be raised to dining height when needed. Built-in furniture and storage walls are well planned to conserve space. The bathroom has a translucent wall over a sunken tub; one of the panes becomes a door opening into a lawn patio for sun bathing in full privacy. A planting scheme for enhancing house and privacy is being gradually developed.

Richard J. Neutra remarks, "How faith moves a mountain could be the motto for this small house perched on a mountain shelf gouged from the steep slope. The young couple knew what they wanted and they wanted it badly enough so that, in the long run, they overcame all obstacles. An excellent contractor overcame all the difficulties of the unusual site." Mr. Neutra also wished to note the efforts of his staff on this house: Dion Neutra, Benno Fischer, Serge Koschin, John Blanton, Toby Schmidbauer, Donald Polsky, Perry Neuschatz and Gunnar Serneblad.

George and Dorothy Serulnic, a young couple, had their house planned while they were still engaged. Both work in the city. He is a musician, she a minister. The architect notes that, "the owners receive a great deal of relaxation when leaving the hustle and bustle of human activity in the city below, and enjoy the peaceful landscape spread below them."

SERULNIC RESIDENCE, Los Angeles, California. Owners: *George and Dorothy Serulnic.* Architect: *Richard J. Neutra.* Contractor: *Fordyce S. Marsh.*

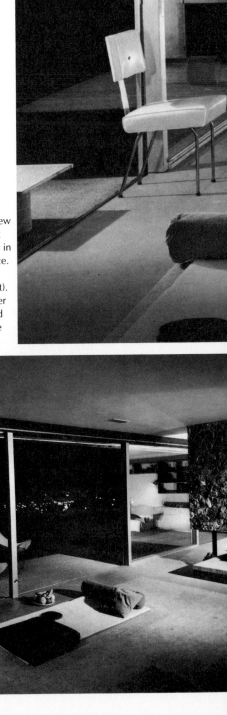

Perhaps the most dramatic view from the Serulnic house is at night (below). Note light strip in overhang to illuminate terrace. Glass walls slide into frame extending beyond house (left). The house has cement plaster finish outside, birch plywood and plaster inside. Floors are concrete.

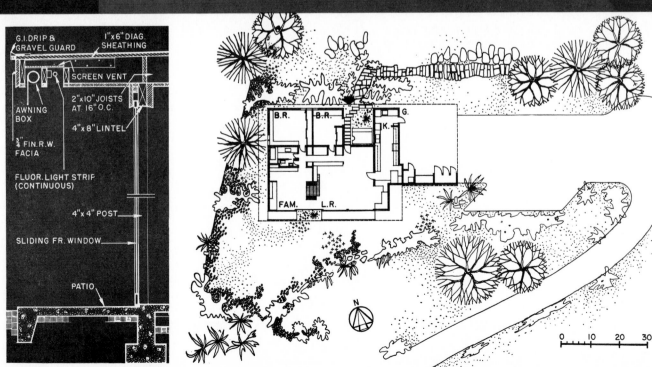

G.I. DRIP &
GRAVEL GUARD

1"x6" DIAG.
SHEATHING

SCREEN VENT

AWNING
BOX

2"x10" JOISTS
AT 16" O.C.

4"x8" LINTEL

3/4" FIN. R.W.
FACIA

FLUOR. LIGHT STRIP
(CONTINUOUS)

4"x4" POST

SLIDING FR. WINDOW

PATIO

B.R.   B.R.   G.

K.

FAM.   L.R.

N

0   10   20   30

P.M. Bolton Associates
Houston, Texas

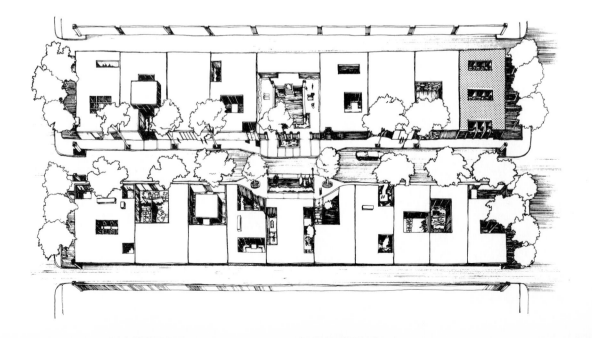

1963

The traditional "townhouse" concept has been successfully revived in this southern house, one of a group of custom-designed row houses for a Houston development planned by the architect. Stylistically, the houses are all quite contemporary, but the use of similar and fairly traditional materials gives a unified, almost "timeless" quality.

The development is built in the midst of a typical city subdivision which has large lawns and traditional houses built out to 10 foot restriction lines at the sides of each lot. By planning this new development as a unit, it was possible to extend the encompassing walls of each house to the lot lines. A communal swimming pool and recreation pavilion are placed at the center of the development. Service alleys range the back of each block of houses.

This house is built on a corner lot of the area, on a site measuring 45 by 75 feet. To minimize the space required, a carport was devised for parking sideways at the back, off the service alley. Vistas are provided for each room inside the house by a series of patios formed by colonnades of brick arches. The arches carry through the house as a design motif.

Architect and owner: Preston M. Bolton. *Location:* Houston, Texas. *Structural Engineer:* R. George Cunningham. *Contractor:* Stewart & Stewart Construction Company.

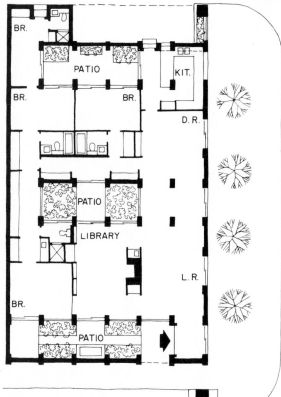

Behind the 12-foot-high paneled doors at the entrance of the Bolton house lies a series of rooms with a startling sense of spaciousness—a quality which is unfortunately not adequately conveyed by the photographs. The owners state that: "People are continually amazed that we have four bedrooms and four baths, each with its own patio view in this limited space, but the living area of our house has been considerably increased by the garden courts. We have small bedrooms and this is the way we like to live—with a minimum of furniture and maximum use of organized dressing room storage. Our favorite place is the library with its walls of books and glass: one way we look out on a patio with a fountain of playing water; the other way, to a tropical garden with swaying palms. We like our house and wouldn't change a thing."

The interior organization of the house is also a very conveniently and flexibly arranged one. For example, the library is placed where it may be used with the living area for entertaining, or with the master bedroom to form a private apartment. The library and living room are divided by a fireplace enclosed in natural

finish walnut with white divider strips.

The kitchen is placed for direct service in the living-dining area or the rear patio, and adjoins the carport to ease the handling of groceries and deliveries. The maid's quarters at the back also have an entrance through the rear patio, which doubles in function as a children's play area. The child's bedroom, bath and dressing room open both from the maid's room and the master bedroom corridor to afford surveillance. The fourth bedroom, bath and dressing room, forms a guest suite. Along the side of the house flanking the public street, are a series of arched windows, shielded by walnut shutters to allow complete privacy or openness, as one desires.

The structure of the house is wood

Edward A. Bourdon photos

frame on a concrete slab, with exterior walls of champagne-colored Mexican brick and concrete block. Interior walls are white-painted wall board, brick and walnut paneling; floors are dark oak with borders of white tile.

Anshen & Allen
San Rafael, California
1956

The decorative quality of exposed structural elements has been made a very dramatic feature in this San Rafael, California, house. With no trace of quaintness or gaudiness, natural materials and a simple, modular post and beam structure give the house an exuberant vitality. The long ranges of free-standing posts form colonnades for divisions between galleries and living areas. For all the openness, individual areas still retain an amazing degree of privacy.

Architects Anshen and Allen were commissioned by Builder Herbert A. Crocker to design a distinctive home, and include all appliances, a $12,000 lot, landscaping, and architects' fees, to be sold at a pre-determined price of $39,500. This spacious, economical design is the result.

The house is located in the Green Valley Country Club Tract, on the outskirts of San Rafael, California. It is a residential development, with generous lots bordering on a golf course. The area is surrounded by the wooded Solano and Napa County hills. There is an acre of land, flat near the street. This area was used as the actual building site. Behind the house, the land rolls up to a tree-covered hill crest. The street lies to the north of the plot.

The open planning, and the gable roof of exposed post and beam construction, provide

The economical device of using exposed construction for architectural effect gives this house unusual distinction. High windows in the redwood front give privacy from the street, while the back is open wide to terrace.

Photo: Rondal Partridge

a fine sense of spaciousness in the house. Variation in the roof height helps suggest room separations, and gives low hanging eaves for sun protection. Openings in the roof over entry and terrace help daylight living areas. All major rooms open onto the terrace, and together, form an immense area for entertaining. An all-purpose family room adjoins the kitchen, and is used for regular meals and lounging. The small living room is used for formal dining. An attic room is over the garage, which has space for a workshop.

This house had the unusual circumstance of satisfying two "clients"—the builder, Mr. Crocker, as the primary client, and Dr. Arons, who bought it, as the ultimate one. As such, it had to reflect the needs of a typical-sized family in the best possible way.

Anshen and Allen note that, "Our actual client for this house was the builder, and the problem that of designing a spacious, attractive house, to be sold at a modest price. Architecturally, the solution required the development of a simple overall form and structural system, with all architectural interest being created within this economical framework."

Herbert A. Crocker responds, "Through the courtesy of the Arons, we were able to show the house to the public. Customers were impressed with the unique but practical design of the home, and in most cases 'appraised' the value of the package at $10–15,000 over the actual price. We feel that this result was achieved through a happy combination of builder and architect's talent and experience."

Dr. and Mrs. J. Arons state, "We visited the house when it was only halfway completed. We fell in love with the location, the lot, the plan of the house and the wonderful feeling of great spaciousness that such an open plan seems to create. Since we moved into the house, we have found every moment a delightful experience."

ARONS RESIDENCE, San Rafael, California. Owners: *Mr. and Mrs. J. Arons.* Architects: *Anshen and Allen.* Engineer: *Robert O. Dewell.* Developer and contractor: *Herbert A. Crocker & Co.*

Photos: Roger Sturtevant

A simple roof, with no jogs, covers the entire house. Most hallways are eliminated by the open gallery. The multi-purpose room (below, center) has its own bath. Interiors are mahogany, redwood, fir ceilings. Heating is by a two-zoned perimeter system.

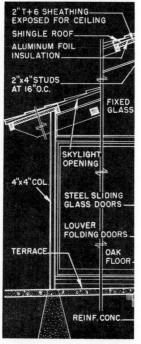

2" T+6 SHEATHING
EXPOSED FOR CEILING

SHINGLE ROOF

ALUMINUM FOIL
INSULATION

2"x4"STUDS
AT 16"O.C.

FIXED
GLASS

SKYLIGHT
OPENING

4"x 4" COL.

STEEL SLIDING
GLASS DOORS

LOUVER
FOLDING DOORS

TERRACE

OAK
FLOOR

REINF. CONC.

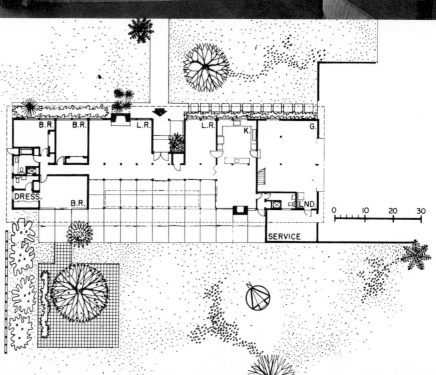

B.R.   B.R.   L.R.   L.R.   K.   G.

DRESS.

B.R.

SERVICE

LND.

0   10   20   30

Nims & Browne
Palm Island, Florida
1956

By simply screening-in a patio and pool area behind this house for Mr. and Mrs. A. E. Miller, Architects Rufus Nims and Robert B. Browne have seemingly doubled the house size, both in appearance and living area. It is not a large house; there are three bedrooms and an all-purpose living area. But the impression is one of tremendous, and luxurious size.

The screened cage encourages outdoor living by keeping out insects, which are a serious problem in the summer months. It is supported by vertical posts, a beam around the top, and cables.

The structure of the house also contributes to the sense of spaciousness by permitting a very open plan. It consists of three flat concrete slabs, 6½ inches thick, supported by fourteen poured concrete columns. The columns are extensions of pilings, required by soil conditions, which rest on bearing rock about fifteen feet below grade. The rigid structure permits partitions to be placed where desired, and to be of light materials—wood louvers, iron grills, glass—which support no weight.

Palm Island lies in Miami Bay, with principal views and breezes to the southeast—over the bay, to the causeway, and beyond to the ocean. Directly beyond the causeway, in the channel to Miami port, there is a dramatic vista of ocean liners steaming in and out. The lot is 100 by 300 feet deep, located on the south side of Palm Island, and facing the southeast. The site required considerable filling. There were no trees, the landscaping was almost totally

The Miller house shows a very fresh use of many familiar materials: concrete, wooden railings, iron grillwork, and above all, screening.

Photos: © Ezra Stoller

brought in. There is a good view of the Miami skyline to the southwest.

A completely open plan for the ground floor, including kitchen, dining, living and patio areas, provides an enormous area for entertaining and relaxed living. The cooking portions of the kitchen are actually in the living area so that the "chef" for the day can still be a part of the party. A separate alcove for cleaning up and washing dishes permits these operations to be done out of sight.

Circulation to the upstairs and from room to room is mostly by means of outside corridors—possible in Florida. Their arrangement, however, would permit them to be closed in. Louvers along top and bottom of balconies reduce glare from sky and water, yet allow air circulation.

Rufus Nims and Robert B. Browne note that, "One of the nice things about our area, we feel, is the lushness of the growth which surrounds us. There has been a conscious effort in this house to make all rooms enjoy an inward extension of this exterior lushness, without sacrificing the psychic necessity of feeling sheltered."

Mr. and Mrs. A. E. Miller have a son, aged 15. They have lived in Miami for a number of years, but came from the north originally. Mr. Miller is an executive in the Howard Johnson Restaurant chain. Both Mr. and Mrs. Miller enjoy cooking as a hobby, and are skilled cooks. They entertain frequently and informally, and required a house especially suitable for large groups of guests. The Millers feel that their house has solved the problem of living in this kind of climate for them very well—and they appreciate this the most. The house allows them to live informally and graciously with comparatively little effort. Mrs. Miller claims that the house requires almost no housekeeping.

MILLER RESIDENCE, Palm Island, Florida. Owners: *Mr. and Mrs. A. E. Miller.* Architects: *Rufus Nims and Robert E. Browne.* Structural engineers: *H. J. Ross and Associates.* Landscape architect: *Jens Koch.* Contractor: *Roger B. Hall.*

The screened enclosure of the patio in the Miller house makes it seem an actual, contained part of the living area (below left). At the far end are the kitchen cooking and clean-up centers (below). The front of the house (right) clearly reveals its concrete column and slab structure.

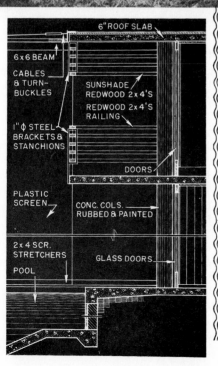

6" ROOF SLAB

6 x 6 BEAM

CABLES
& TURN-
BUCKLES

SUNSHADE
REDWOOD 2 x 4'S

REDWOOD 2 x 4'S
RAILING

1" Ø STEEL
BRACKETS &
STANCHIONS

DOORS

PLASTIC
SCREEN

CONC. COLS.
RUBBED & PAINTED

2 x 4 SCR.
STRETCHERS

GLASS DOORS

POOL

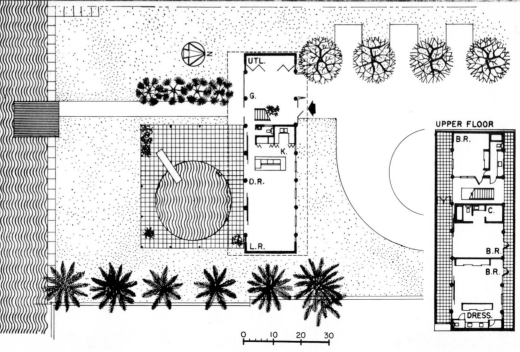

UTL.

G.

K.

D.R.

L.R.

UPPER FLOOR

B.R.

C.

B.R.

B.R.

DRESS.

0   10   20   30

Barbara and Julian Neski
East Hampton   1972
New York

At first glance, the plan of the Stephen Kaplan house in Easthampton, New York may seem no more than a modish exercise in diagonal geometry. Two characteristics of the site, however, make it work very well indeed. First, it is set in a landscape nursery whose shrubs and trees have a strong linear pattern. The vertical lines on the plan (opposite) relate to that geometry. Second, the major diagonals, especially in the family-living room wing, are parallel to the prevailing breezes. In August, when everyone else has closed up the windows and switched on the air conditioner, this house is full of gently moving air. Barbara and Julian Neski have played with that openness in visual terms as well. The angular, rather massive facade that visitors approach from the south literally dissolves into a space (overpage) so filled with light that it hardly seems enclosed at all. The substantial exterior forms of bleached cedar siding contrast with a white interior that has two enormous triangular skylights. One of them can be seen (above) casting afternoon shadows high on the living room wall.

Architects: BARBARA AND JULIAN NESKI. Owners: Mr. and Mrs. Stephen Kaplan. Location: Easthampton, New York. Engineers: Stanley Gleit (structural); Weber & Grahn (mechanical). Contractor: Peter Wazlo.

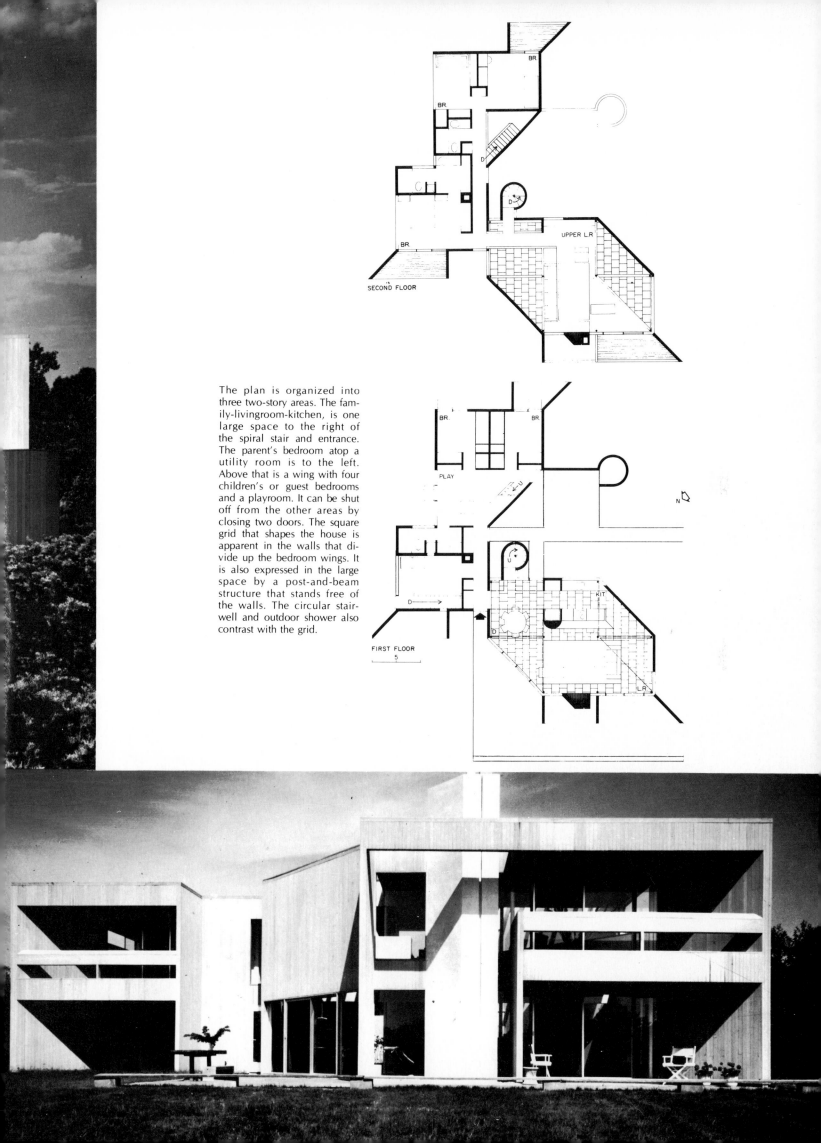

SECOND FLOOR

BR.

BR.

BR.

BR.

UPPER L.R.

The plan is organized into three two-story areas. The family-livingroom-kitchen, is one large space to the right of the spiral stair and entrance. The parent's bedroom atop a utility room is to the left. Above that is a wing with four children's or guest bedrooms and a playroom. It can be shut off from the other areas by closing two doors. The square grid that shapes the house is apparent in the walls that divide up the bedroom wings. It is also expressed in the large space by a post-and-beam structure that stands free of the walls. The circular stairwell and outdoor shower also contrast with the grid.

BR.

BR.

PLAY

N

KIT.

D

LR.

FIRST FLOOR
5

The stairway in the children's wing (left), with open risers and a solid baluster, is a playful switch on usual practice. The white door at the head of the stairs and the one beneath separate the children completely from the rest of the house when that is desired. The parent's bedroom (above) has its own large balcony. It is near the children yet connects, by a bridge, directly to the upper level sitting area in the family-living room wing and to the first floor by the circular stair.

William Maris

"The family-living room wing is meant to be an active, dynamic light-filled space; the system of columns, beams, skylights, open wells and glass combine to provide a setting for family activity and entertaining on two levels," say the Neskis. Four views from differing heights and positions within the space testify to the excitement of the room. The upper area Is meant to be used for quieter entertaining in conjunction with the parent's suite.

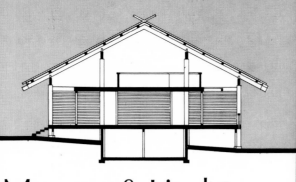

Morgan & Lindstrom
Bainbridge Island Washington
1979

The high quality design of this unique contemporary residence lies with the coalescence of forms and materials. The site is on Bainbridge Island, one of the largest islands in Puget Sound off Seattle; it is heavily wooded with some views to the waterfront. The house was set between two large stands of trees to maximize its isolation from nearby traffic and to permit sunlight to directly hit the entire house. As a bonus, an open children's play yard was created, and it, too, is filled with sunlight.

Called a "structure within a structure" by the architects, an all wood frame supports a superimposed roof, under which is shielded enclosed living quarters. The frame is composed of 24 heavy timber posts and four main beams; a large 7,000-square-foot roof is totally covered with translucent fiberglass roof panels. The integrated "understructure," clad in cedar siding, has a pristine appearance and sharp outline that accentuates the visual strength of horizontal and vertical lines.

The design of the super structure is primarily for visual effect—as the sunlight strikes it, the entire roof lights up, for the translucent roof panels diffuse the sunlight, giving the appearance of a very light and airy structure.

While there is some design influence from structures built by the Northwest American Indians seen in the use of massive timber poles and the cross-bracing at the apex of the gable, an Oriental influence is overpowering. An external spatial sequence exists, from open area, to white-colored rock bordering the pavilion-like building, to an elevated deck, to the great roof. Details of the deck walkway (top right) and the main entrance (bottom right) demonstrate the almost ceremonial procession into the interiors.

LINDSTROM RESIDENCE, Bainbridge Island, Washington. Architects: *Morgan and Lindstrom.* Contractor: *Walt Johnsen Construction.*

Photos: Christian Staub

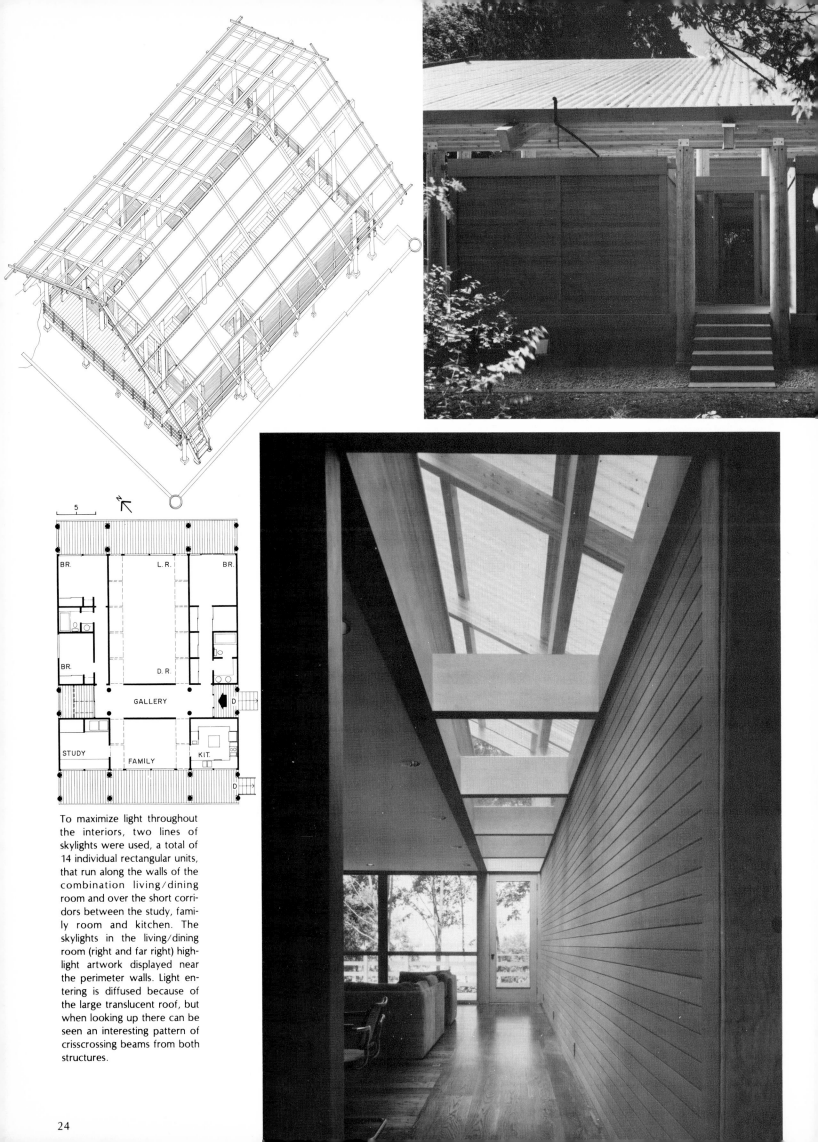

To maximize light throughout the interiors, two lines of skylights were used, a total of 14 individual rectangular units, that run along the walls of the combination living/dining room and over the short corridors between the study, family room and kitchen. The skylights in the living/dining room (right and far right) highlight artwork displayed near the perimeter walls. Light entering is diffused because of the large translucent roof, but when looking up there can be seen an interesting pattern of crisscrossing beams from both structures.

On two sides of the house, there is an open veranda. The main entrance (left) is not, however, positioned off the front deck but rather on the side, connecting to a broad interior gallery, off which all rooms flow. Unifying the interiors with the identical exterior material, cedar paneling was specified and timber posts were exposed to tie-in the superstructure as well as continue a processional pattern of spaces established outside. Views to the woods are available from the kitchen (right), family, study and laundry rooms; views to the waterfront are from bedrooms and living/dining area (below).

Paul Rudolph
New York City   1970

Paul Rudolph has introduced a number of spatial and planning innovations and surprises into his design for this New York townhouse. Behind an elegantly disciplined, and somewhat sober facade (brown-painted steel set with obscure, brown, structural glass panels), one enters into a skillfully lighted, white-gray-black series of spaces that culminate in a big, 27-foot-high living area backed by a three-story greenhouse. Level changes, balconies, open stairs, and tidily integrated fittings abound, in Rudolph's typical fashion, to create a lot of variety and in-

FIRST FLOOR

SECOND FLOOR

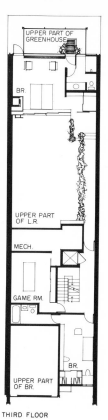

THIRD FLOOR

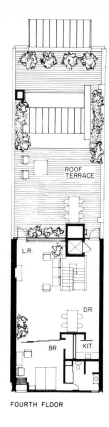

FOURTH FLOOR

Privacy is assured throughout the house by obscured glass panels on the front, and a narrow greenhouse at the back. Inside, however, the effect is one of openness, brightness and light.

terest in a very cohesive series of spaces.

The house was built on the existing frame of an 1870 coach house, which originally had three floors. A fourth level was achieved in the new house, and within the original space, by creating a mezzanine for the master bedroom suite and its adjoining sitting-room balcony.

The usual back garden—one of the great pleasures in a townhouse—has been raised to the top level; greenery and a great sense of openness have been introduced into the living area by skylights and the tall greenhouse. Mirrored walls line the lower portions of the greenhouse to augment the effect and the apparent depth. A balcony-bedroom (which can be closed by folding panels) also overlooks the greenhouse, and is connected by a bridge to the game room level. An open stair connects the living area with the master bedroom suite, and an elevator and a central stair connect all levels.

Floors on the entire first level are surfaced with black slate, and the slate is continued around the dropped living room area as a sill for sitting or counter space.

A quiet color scheme and a minimum number of different materials provide a counterfoil to the vigorous changes of level in the big living area. Balconies and bridges extend into the space to create extra usable areas. Stairs are kept to a minimal center support and treads; the slate landing of the stair at right extends to form a mantel for the fireplace.

Floors in all other areas are covered with gray carpet, with the exception of baths, which are white marble or ceramic tile.

With a lot of the seating and storage built into the house, other furnishings are kept to a minimum, and carefully selected or designed to add to the overall spatial effect. Materials and fabrics are generally kept in the same monochrome color scheme (white-gray-black) as the house, with accents of glass, clear plastic and silver to add sparkle; plants, books and works of art give bright color relief.

Architect: PAUL RUDOLPH
54 West 57th Street, New York City
Townhouse
Location: New York City
Interior design: Paul Rudolph
Contractor: Blitman Corporation

Erickson/Massey
Cotuit, Mass. 1969

This summer home, designed for lighting consultant William M. C. Lam, gains an added cachet as the first U.S. project by architect Arthur Erickson of Vancouver—and therefore, the first of his houses eligible for a Record Houses award. Although not an expensive house (the cost was about $36,000), it has the same elegance, ease and power of the larger houses he has done in Canada. And, most important, owner Lam is pleased: "Unlike much of contemporary architecture, in which structure is displayed as a feature itself, Erickson's dramatic structures shape views, define spaces (rather than modules), and are a powerful yet subtle means of unifying complex combinations of spaces with numerous changes in levels. The quiet Cape shore views are given excitement when juxtaposed with the heavy framework of 6-by-16 rough fir beams and posts."

In a basic bi-nuclear scheme dividing living and sleeping spaces, the architect has used the post and beam framework to exuberantly link a variety of outdoor spaces with the interiors, and to carefully frame views in a manner reminiscent of classic Japanese architecture—of which Erickson is reportedly a great student. In a very interested student. In one (the enclosed spaces are tinted on the plan), but the close integration with outdoor living areas gives a sense of great spaciousness. There is also a detached guest house (not shown) with its own kitchenette, bath, deck and outdoor areas.

The exteriors and interiors have rough red cedar walls; the roof is built-up, floors are re-sawn fir, and partitions are dry-wall. With this as background, all the other interior finishes and furnishings are kept simple to reflect a summer house.

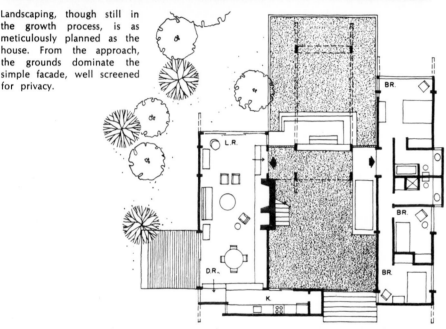

Landscaping, though still in the growth process, is as meticulously planned as the house. From the approach, the grounds dominate the simple facade, well screened for privacy.

LAM RESIDENCE, Cotuit, Massachusetts. Owners: *Mr. and Mrs. William M. C. Lam*. Architect: *Arthur Erickson of Erickson/Massey*—job captain: *Fred Dalla-Lana*. Lighting: *William M. C. Lam*. Engineer: *Brogue Babicki*. Contractor: *John B. Lebel*.

Court, gallery, terrace and deck form a succession of different outdoor living spaces. There is also a "project area and lower court"—a sheltered space below the bedroom block for rainy-day activities.

The living/dining room (above) is enlarged by planned vistas and decks. The kitchen is separated from the area by serving counters only, to increase the informal spaciousness; it also adjoins the central court.

31

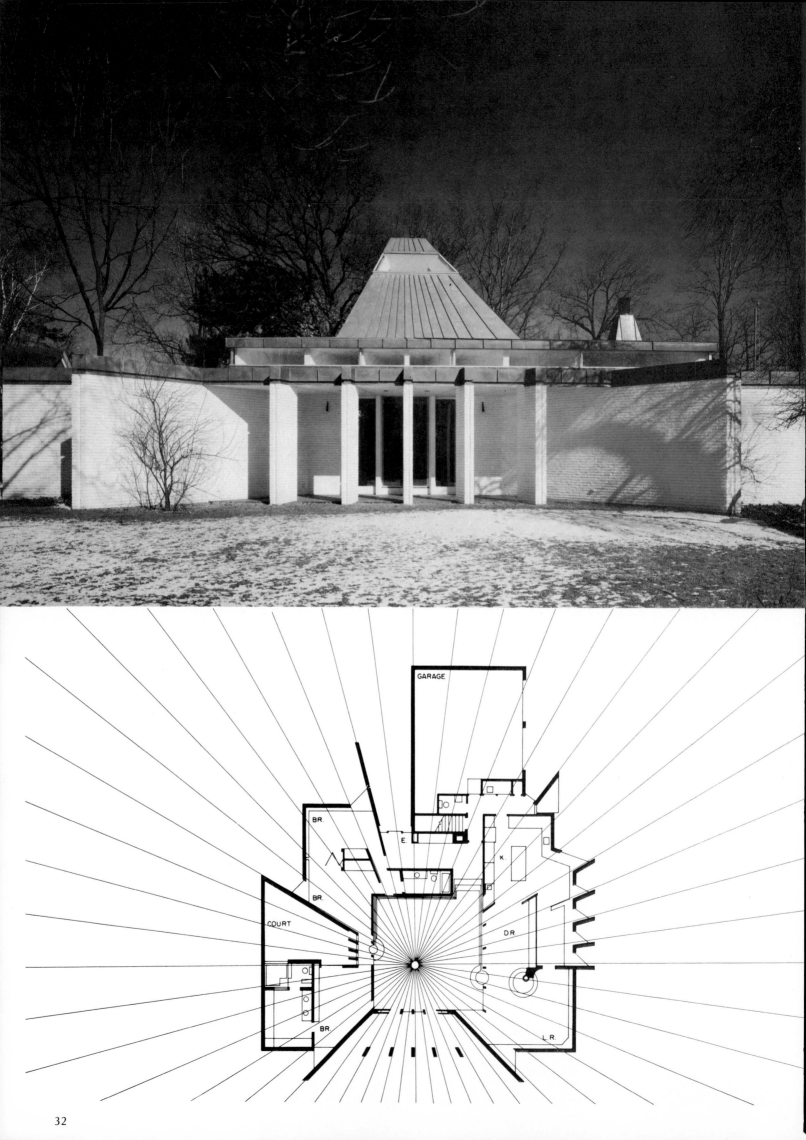

GARAGE

BR.

BR.

COURT

BR.

E.

K.

DR.

L.R.

Gunnar Birkerts & Associates
Grand Rapids, Michigan
1968

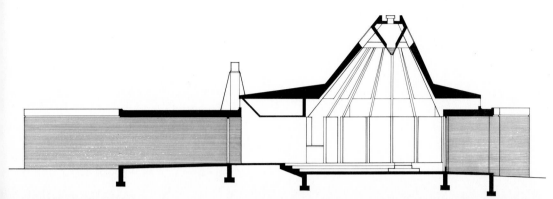

Bill Engdahl, Hedrich-Blessing photos

Variety of experience in spaces and lighting is a quality much talked about, but too seldom achieved in today's houses; Gunnar Birkerts has achieved it in this moderate-sized house by using a strong and all-pervading design idea. The house, which is located on a rather limited, but beautifully wooded site within the city limits, has a plan concept which evolved from the owner's desire to have an atrium-like "introverted" central space. From this requirement, Birkerts has evolved a highly intellectualized, radial plan and structure, which permits a choice of totally open or mostly closed (but always well defined) spaces, all tinctured by an unusual and constantly changing play of light.

As Birkerts puts it, "all surrounding spaces radiate out of an eccentric center in the atrium (a small bronze square marks the spot in the photo at left) and open directly on it at varying degrees. Dining and living areas are permanently open to the atrium space; however, the kitchen and bedroom areas can be taken in visually by opening hinged panels in the walls. Opposite every viewing panel in the atrium is a glazed opening in the exterior wall. Thus vistas are developed which extend and expand the visual depth, and allow one to experience the total house. Exterior windows are positioned in a way that prevents outsiders from looking directly into the rooms, but light is reflected into all spaces from angled walls."

The bouncing light created by these windows is everywhere augmented by clerestories and skylights, and often baffled by deep, structural "chambers" to create the needed variety of shades and shadows. Other than its radial concept, the structure is a conventional one, of durable, quality materials: wood stud, brick, marble or carpeted floors, lead-coated copper roof.

PRIVATE RESIDENCE, Grand Rapids, Michigan. Architects: *Gunnar Birkerts & Associates.* Mechanical engineers: *Hoyem, Basso & Adams.* Contractor: *Jordan Sheperd, Inc.*

In this well-equipped, comfortable house, Gunnar Birkerts has provided more-than-ample built-in units for basic storage needs. The owners were thus required to add only a near-minimum of furnishings: strong "decorative" quality is inherent in the house itself.

The central atrium functions as "living space"—a separated short entrance hall links front and service doors with this big, central hall, and with the garage, kitchen and children's rooms.

As noted before, panels that swing or slide create many varied spatial or visual effects: between dining room and kitchen (top right); as a pass-through between atrium and kitchen (above); and even into bedrooms (left and far right) from the atrium.

Exterior fenestration is also varied for interior needs and privacy; the entrance side is relatively closed (bottom right), while the kitchen areas are banked with angled, view-obscuring windows (center right).

SECOND FLOOR   5

FIRST FLOOR

BR.

KIT.   L.R.

OPEN   BR.

BR.   OPEN

KIT.

L.R.

MLTW/Moore Turnbull
Monterey, California
1967

A three-story-high vertical living space transforms this simple-appearing, shingle-clad house into quarters for a very relaxed way of life. The architects state that "the owners had tired of their large conventional house, and were anxious to spend their limited budget on the excitement usually associated with a vacation house, rather than on the fixtures and appliances ordinarily expected in a house for year-round living." The resulting house thus minimizes "service" aspects (there is a wall-kitchen), and concentrates on a riot of color, space, comfort, books, music, and a balcony which serves as a quiet sitting nook, and occasionally as a stage for theatricals and a place to hold a band for parties.

The owners, Mr. and Mrs. Karas, are a couple whose children are grown. Thus "zoning" was not as important as in a house for a larger family; living space, in effect runs throughout the house, wheeling around the little service core on the first floor, and rising to the high shed roof. There are two principal bedrooms and a bath on the second level; on the third level is a loft, reached by a ladder, for visiting children.

A "sun scoop" is employed in the Karas house to gain extra light on the pine-forested site, which is often foggy and sunless. Over one of the larger, upper windows in the living space, a "white baffle with an enormous yellow sun painted on it is enlisted to bounce south light into the house and to warm up the atmosphere within to a surprising degree", according to the architects.

A lower-ceilinged portion of the first floor living area is dominated by a large fireplace, which was cast in sand on the floor of the house by the contractor. This area has been treated as a smaller, cozier retreat, as contrasted with the taller reaches of other parts of the room. The furnishings of the house, many of which are built-in, are simple and sturdy, and rely for effect on bright splashes of color and a liberal sprinkling of handcraft accessories. As its original program has intended, the house does lend itself to a sort of perpetual vacation life—and in a remarkable and very different way.

KARAS RESIDENCE, Monterey, California. Owners: *Mr. and Mrs. Sam Karas.* Architects: *Charles W. Moore and William Turnbull, Jr. of MLTW/Moore Turnbull.* Engineer: *Patrick Morreau of Davis & Morreau Associated.* Contractor: *Douglas S. Chandler.*

Photos: © 1967 Morley Baer

"Well, all I asked for was a roof over my head."

2. EXPERIMENTS WITH STRUCTURE

Inseparable from the space/cost quandaries in designing houses are the natures of the supporting structure and enclosing materials. Ironically, though there had been momentous developments in materials and structural engineering for the previous hundred years, well into the 1940s most American houses were still built more or less as they long had been: the hand-made, wood stud-frame sheathed with clapboards, or load-bearing and finish walls of brick or stone. There were many exceptions, of course. Shingles, stucco, tiles and other largely regional finishes were used, and there were some uses, usually carefully concealed, of concrete and steel. And there had been flirtations with such then new materials as glass block, aluminum and plywood. The Great Depression led to some tentative attempts to reduce costs, such as using tamped earth, and at prefabricating houses or their parts. But in general, there was not much experimentation.

A major part of the problem was a limited conception in the public mind of what a house should look like. That this should be generally true in the United States at mid-century is somewhat of a paradox—what with the incredibly mixed heritage of people from everywhere, bringing widely divergent patterns of living and building; the broad range of climate, terrain and materials in the country; and a diverse history of the American house from log cabin to hacienda, from open southern plantation styles to northern redoubts against the winters. And the latter part of the 19th and early 20th century was a ferment of house styles and experiments.

The pressing need for new houses in the late 1940s brought a building boom that helped re-kindle an adventurous esthetic spirit. In the midst of the ubiquitous "accepted" styles, houses were being built by inventive architects across the U.S. that didn't necessarily look like a house in common parlance, but used all sorts of structural materials, finishes and methods to open the horizons of what a liveable, contemporary house *could* look like.

There was the added impetus of the move to the U.S. by many of Europe's most talented architects: Walter Gropius, Mies van der Rohe, Marcel Breuer, Richard Neutra, Serge Chermayeff, Eliel Saarinen, Josep Luis Sert among them. The admix of their varied visions and those of native American architects brought about a creative era that has focused the world's attention on houses in the U.S. for three decades. In time, it will, without doubt, be regarded as one of the truly great periods in the history of residential architecture. Yet it represents no single, concise "international" or "modern" style, but many fresh, contemporary styles—from many roots, with many flowerings.

Most every material that could possibly be used to construct a house was experimented with and each evolved its own look, its own esthetic. Superlative designs made common materials respectable: concrete block, corrugated metal, plywoods, plastics. Industrial and technological advances were incorporated as they became readily available, and the cost permitted: long steel cantilevers, space frames, laminated arches, concrete slabs and shaped roofs, great areas of insulating and sun-screening glass.

Serious studies were made to reconcile the planning of houses with the standard sizes of manufactured materials and parts—from bricks, plywood panels, wallboards, timber lengths, steel beams, to complete roof trusses, window units, doors, "sandwich panel" walls, cabinets and equipment. The use of medium-scale modules of three or four feet and ranging down to the small four-inch increments of "modular coordination" helped reduce the time and costs of designing and construction. And manufacturers helped by coordinating their standards and introducing new products.

Hand-in-hand with the modular concept—and with the desire for more open, flexible planning—was the widespread development of the post and beam structure for houses. With origins buried in antiquity, it was latterly resurrected by Mies

"He broke the box alright—if that's any consolation."

AND FORMS

in his stunning, but incredibly costly, chrome-plated "star columns" for the pavilion he designed for the Barcelona Exposition of 1929, and also in his and Le Corbusier's use of cheaper, painted steel lally columns. Posts and beams in wood, or steel, made possible the use of non–load-bearing curtain walls of a wide variety of lightweight materials to enclose houses, and freely permitted partitioning in any fashion desired. From individually designed houses, post and beam construction gradually evolved into a popular development-type house known—for some inexplicable reason—as "ranch house style."

While the most obvious form for such houses was low and horizontal with a flat roof, there were multitudes of variations combining butterfly, shed and pitched roofs, with flat sections to produce many variations in shape and form.

Other long-span materials and methods brought more differing forms to houses. Reinforced concrete was shaped into vaults, "bubbles" and boxes. Laminated plywoods were formed into arched and parabolic curves. Steel and other metals permitted light tent, umbrella, folded plate and other unfa-

miliar but obviously associative appearances. Concrete block and brick were transmuted from heavy solidity into new skylines of light, open geometrics. And different materials were combined in new ways in the same structure.

Far from the "catalog architecture" sameness that many predicted from the use of standardized, industrial materials, exuberant houses were created in a plethora of never-before-seen forms and styles in rapid succession. Too many and too fast, perhaps, for easy assimilation—and perhaps, as with the totally open plan, not all are suited to everyone. There are the bold and the inherently quiet.

But the machine-made house has been a taunting lure ever since the industrial revolution, and there have been many sallies into trying to achieve it. Though such schemes as the government's dream of Detroit-like assembly-line mass production of houses in "Operation Breakthrough" came to little, standardized houses built in prefabricated sections, and highly individual houses made of a variety of machine-made parts are firm realities—and significant cost-savers. And, of course, there are all those mobile homes. All in all, the belief that 20th-century technology and engineering made almost anything possible in house design and construction *had* to be tested—and, by and large, was.

The crisp stamp of the machine, however, is not universally overt in the contemporary houses of the past few decades. Similar materials, handled differently, have been used to create a soft-spoken warmth: in the wood houses of the Northwest, in the stone and wood houses of Marcel Breuer and Herbert Beckhard, in the brick and glass houses of Preston Bolton, in the multi–shed-roofed "woodland" houses of Edward Larrabee Barnes, to cite only a few.

The "nature of materials" has been almost exhaustively explored, tested, refined—and has, in its variety and ingenuity, vastly enlarged our concept of "house," adding many fresh, ever-applicable ideas to our traditions.

"How does he ever expect to be an architect if he can't invent a new roof?"

Paul Rudolph
St. John's County
Florida

1963

One of the uniquely different designs among Record Houses is this one with its very sculptural use of concrete block. The exterior of the house is dominated by the powerful composition of rectangles forming a sunshade across the rear facade (shown above in the original sketch and completed structure). The spirit of this wall is continued on to the interior of the house, where the floors are arranged on seven different levels.

Comments of the owners, after having lived in the house for some time, are worth noting: "We knew enough of Mr. Rudolph's previous works to know that the end result would correspond to our ideas of beauty . . . (and) our faith in the architect was well placed. We are extremely fond of the house. Externally, it is a beautiful piece of sculpture—blending graciously with the sea and the sand surrounding it. It is very comforting inside . . . different ceiling heights, different views, different floor levels make it always interesting, always varied."

The house is a very spacious and conveniently arranged one. All the living areas are essentially one room, with areas for dining, sitting by the fireplace, and the like, created principally by changes in the floor levels. The hallway linking the upstairs bedrooms is treated as a balcony, and adds yet another level to this varied space. As a counterfoil, colors and other decoration are subdued.

As can be noted in these photos of the Milam house, the already big living areas are made to appear even larger and more open by using very few pieces of portable furniture. In fact, about the only ones are the dining table and its seats. Basic seating for conversation and lounging is formed by cushioned units supported by one of the floor levels.

The house is constructed of sand colored concrete block, left exposed inside and out. The main floor is terrazzo, and the second

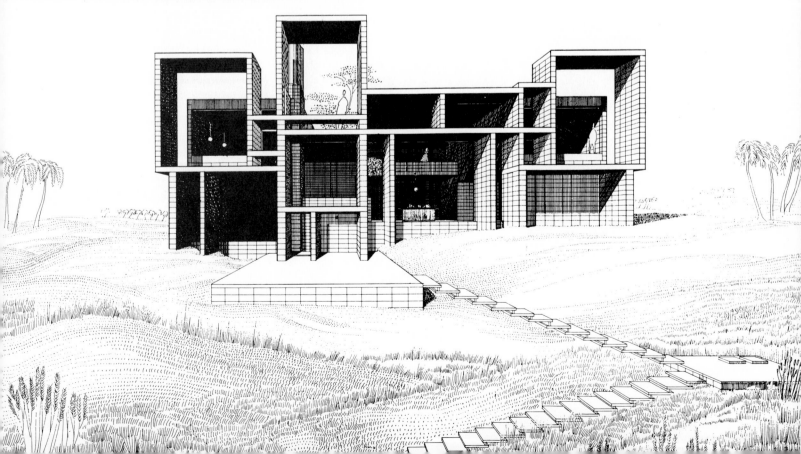

floors are hardwood or carpet except for tile in the bathrooms. Ceilings are acoustical plaster for noise absorption in the big areas. The small windows in the baths are supplemented for daylighting by plastic skylights. One of the baths also has an outside exit and stair to serve as a dressing area for swimmers from the beach. Bedroom closets are provided in the nooks near each entrance.

The kitchen (center right) is conveniently placed for access to the living and dining areas (via a pass through), to the garage for unloading groceries, and to the front door. The entire house is air conditioned. The cost of the house itself was about $88,074.

MILAM RESIDENCE, St. John's County, Florida. Owners: *Mr. and Mrs. Arthur W. Milam*. Architect: *Paul Rudolph—supervising architect: Robert Ernest*. Structural engineer: *Herman Spiegel*. Mechanical engineers: *Frank B. Wilder & Associates*. Contractor: *William E. Arnold Company*.

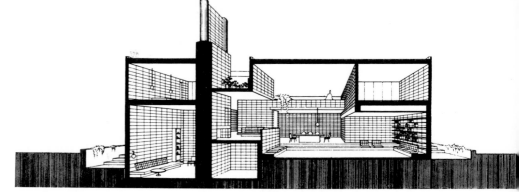

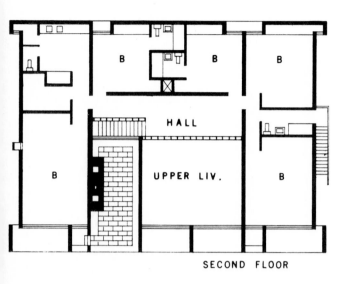

SECOND FLOOR

B · B · B · B

HALL

B · UPPER LIV. · B

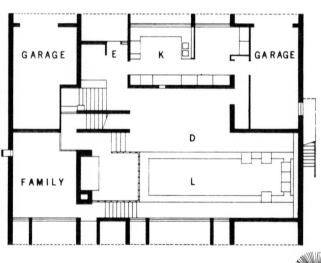

GARAGE · E · K · GARAGE

FAMILY · D · L

0 · 5 · 20

FIRST FLOOR

Photos: Joseph W. Molitor

Philip Johnson
Long Island, New York
1962

The problem of designing a large house for an extremely narrow lot has been solved here by splitting the plan into two pavilions, each offset from the other, with the long axis of each following that of the site. One unit is devoted to living, dining and kitchen, with service quarters below; the other contains bedrooms, library, laundry and storage. The two units are connected by an interior corridor on the lower level, and by an open terrace above (see plan on next page).

The site is 100 feet above a "fjord" type of inlet, and offers very dramatic views. The offset plan of the two pavilions allows views from all rooms—and the major view over the water is capitalized on by the spectacular raised living pavilion shown here. It projects out over the edge of the cliff, giving the effect of being built in the trees, and sheltering a terrace below. The design of this one unit is based on an early sketch of Mies van der Rohe's, with diagonal truss-like members crossing in front of the glass walls.

PRIVATE RESIDENCE, Long Island, New York. Architect: *Philip Johnson*. Structural engineers: *Eipel Engineering*. Mechanical engineer: *Fred S. Dubin*.

Photos: © Ezra Stoller

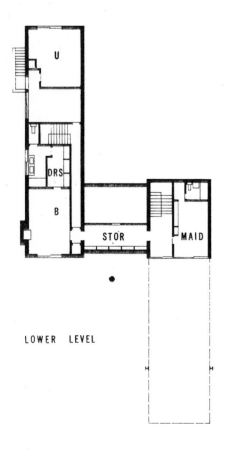

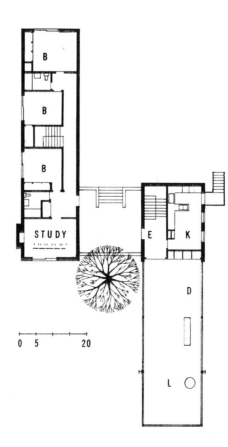

LOWER LEVEL

0 5   20

The plan of this Long Island house gives excellent separation for living and bedroom areas—an especially useful item for the sea-side location where entertaining may be more frequent than in less pleasant locales. The big living area and terraces can accommodate a large number of guests. The structure is a very nicely proportioned one, with a frame of exposed, and painted, structural steel on concrete foundations. Exterior walls are of brick and glass; interiors are painted plaster, on wood studs. All ceilings are plaster except for acoustic tile in the playroom. The roof is built-up tar and gravel. Interiors are simply but well finished. Flooring for the various rooms includes: mosaic tile in living areas, rubber tile in kitchen and playroom, ceramic tile in baths.

Photos: Marc Neuhof

Jules Gregory
Verona, New Jersey   1963

Some truly exciting and dramatic spaces are created in this large house by its roof of laminated arches and solid, curved wood deck. Although roofs of this type have often been seen in religious and other structures, it is a fairly unique application for a residence. Its effect is heightened by the peak skylight.

The house is built on the highest point of land in Montclair, New Jersey, and provides views of New York from the Statue of Liberty to the George Washington Bridge. An ancient, four-story Victorian house was demolished to provide site and foundation for the new structure. The size of the house was thus limited by these existing stone foundations.

The upper level of the house is devoted to the parents' use, with living room, dining room, bedroom, bath and dressing room, and kitchen. The lower floor is for use of the children, with bedrooms, bath, recreation rooms and servants' quarters.

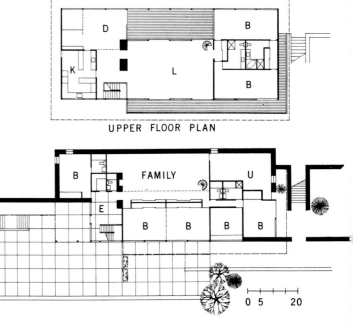

UPPER FLOOR PLAN

D   B
K   L   B

B   FAMILY   U
E
B   B   B   B

0 5   20

The peaked roof of the Gombos house forms a very sympathetic design to crest its elevated site, which falls in a sharp bluff at the rear of the house. The laminated curved members of the roof are set along diagonal lines for bracing purposes, and form a variation of the conventional post and beam construction.

Within the house, the big central living area is opened to the full height of the roof. The smaller rooms flanking this are carefully fitted beneath the arches so that an entirely different, smaller-scaled effect is created. Some of the rooms, such as the bedroom (bottom left), have additional partial ceilings of glass suspended in wood frames at partition height. These are electrically lighted from the top at night, and daylighted by the long central skylight.

On the lower level is a very big recreation room and bar; which doubles as exhibition space for a large part of the owners' collection of very good paintings. Adjoining this area, two of the children's bedrooms are divided by a folding partition, so that this area can be converted into a secondary play space. All the rooms in the house, incidentally, are quite spacious.

Outdoor living spaces are generously provided throughout the house. A big covered deck on the view side runs the entire length of the living room. On the opposite side, looking over the entrance drive and a valley garden, is a balcony running three-quarters of the length of the house, and partially across one end (steps leading from this balcony to the rear lawn were yet to be constructed when the photo, top left, was taken). Many of the splendidly planted original gardens were adapted for the new house, and give a variety of secluded paths and lookout spots.

The exterior of the house is stucco, and the roof is surfaced with asphalt shingles. The interiors are finished with float-finished plaster, and the downstairs are sound conditioned with acoustical tile on the ceilings. Most windows are framed in sliding aluminum sash. The house has a built-in intercommunications and Hi-Fi system.

The kitchen is a very complete and elegantly equipped area, and includes an "island" location for the rangetop which gives access to both sides (bottom right). A secondary sink counter doubles as a bar. The room includes space for a breakfast table and chairs. Floors throughout the house are terrazzo. Bathroom surfaces are tile.

Furnishings in the house are largely oriental pieces collected by the owners and reinforce the eastern flavor of the house.

GOMBOS RESIDENCE, Verona, New Jersey. Architect: *Jules Gregory*. Engineers: *Bliss & Hanle*. Contractor: *Phillip Leone*.

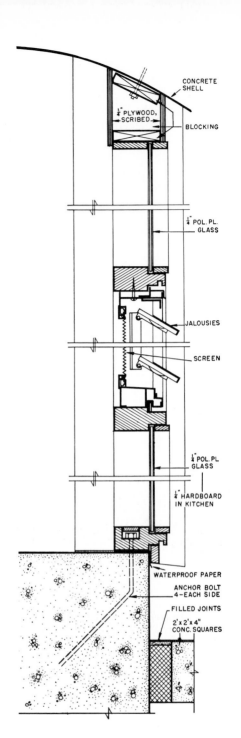

CONCRETE
SHELL

¼" PLYWOOD,
SCRIBED

BLOCKING

¼" POL. PL.
GLASS

JALOUSIES

SCREEN

¼" POL. PL
GLASS

¼" HARDBOARD
IN KITCHEN

WATERPROOF PAPER

ANCHOR BOLT
4 - EACH SIDE

FILLED JOINTS

2' x 2' x 4"
CONC. SQUARES

Photos: E. J. Cyr

Eliot Noyes
Hobe Sound, Florida
1956

The shape of this "bubble" house is not just a capricious whim, but is solidly based on an interesting and practical construction method which uses a balloon as a form for concrete—the patented Airform method, invented by architect Wallace Neff of California just before WWII. The two houses shown here, designed by architect Noyes, are an entirely fresh approach the Airform International Construction Corporation is taking in developing the economical construction system.

A circular concrete foundation is poured,

with reinforcing bars bent into hooks and protruding from the surface. A balloon is spread out on the foundation and attached to a steel cable run through the hooks. The balloon is then inflated, covered with reinforcing, and sprayed with concrete. Pressure is kept constant by a compressor for about twenty-four hours until the concrete is set. The balloon is then deflated and removed. The dome is covered with a vapor seal, glass-fiber insulation, and more reinforcing and a second layer of concrete sprayed on.

Architect Noyes' designs include (left and in section) a 30-foot diameter house in Hobe Sound, Florida; Murphy Construction Company was Contractor. A larger, 60-foot diameter example (above and right) has three bedrooms, two bathrooms, living-dining area and kitchen—a typical arrangement is shown in the model at right.

PRIVATE RESIDENCE, Hobe Sound, Florida. Architect: *Eliot Noyes*. Contractor: *Murphy Construction Company*.

Eliot Noyes

Alfred De Vido
East Hampton, New York
1969

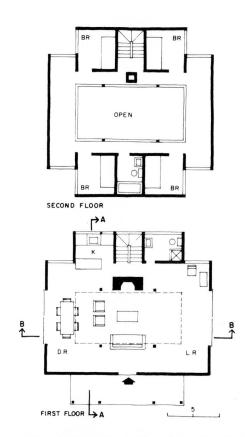

SECOND FLOOR

FIRST FLOOR

This sophisticated little vacation house epitomizes the reaction of city dwellers against the small, standardized rooms of today's apartments, and their strong desire for big, soaring spaces in their second homes in the country. As architect De Vido puts it, "I wanted a large living space— shaped, textured and dramatic— to contrast with the more mundane shapes of apartment living."

He has achieved this in a striking manner, and within an extremely reasonable budget—about $21,000 for the house alone in 1968. The heart of the concept is a big, three-story space, filled with sunlight. At the lower, living levels, this space extends to the outdoors through two sliding glass walls. Four bedrooms, small but adequate, and two fair-sized lounge/bunk areas are on the second or balcony level. At the very top are two aeries, reached by retractable ladders, for work and drafting. Big banks of windows on two sides provide light and views for these platform areas. These spaces, plus two baths and a small, open kitchen, provide most facilities of a very big house.

The house is situated on a long and narrow strip of woodland, and was designed to provide privacy on the two exposures closest to the neighboring lots and views of the woods and flowering shrubs on the other sides. The house is boldly symmetrical, with

the main approach on the center axis, via a covered entrance porch and a path from a parking area.

The design itself is a discerning, rustic understatement, with exposed structural parts and natural wood finishes used throughout. Variation and accent are achieved by texture—cedar shingle outside, rough-sawn cedar walls and polished white pine floors inside—and by a darker stain for the trim. The total effect is one of ease and warmth and freshness.

DE VIDO RESIDENCE, East Hampton, New York. Architect: *Alfred De Vido*. Contractor: *Pete De Castro*.

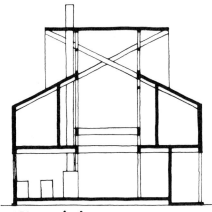 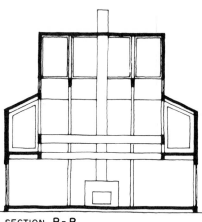

SECTION **A-A**   SECTION **B-B**

The structure consists of a basic Douglas fir post-and-girt system (on a 5-foot module), plus four central columns and "x" trusses to support the highest roof. The exterior wall is insulated, and all glass is insulating, to allow electric heat in winter.

Ulrich Franzen
Essex, Connecticut   1960

In this remarkable house, Architect Franzen develops to a greater degree some of the design hallmarks, for a pavilion house under great soaring roofs, that he started with his own house. In this example, dramatic use was made of a hilltop site to vivify the impression made by the glass pavilion roofed by nine inverted umbrellas, and to exploit to the fullest the surprise of a spectacular view.

The site is a mountain top with panoramic vistas of the Essex River and its yacht basin, Plum Island, and Long Island Sound—with occasional glimpses of Montauk lighthouse. The vistas are not apparent as one drives up to the mountaintop through a mile of woods.

To heighten the effect, the house was developed with a lower level set into the hillside, retained by walls of granite found on the site. This level contains sleeping and service rooms, as well as the entrance hall; it is a quiet area with closed vistas into the woods and toward a pond. The active areas—living room, dining room and kitchen—are placed in the open glass pavilion set above the stone podium. As one enters the house, the experience of walking up into the pavilion and the view is one of increasing surprise and excitement.

PRIVATE RESIDENCE, Essex, Connecticut. Architect: *Ulrich Franzen.* Contractor: *Wilfred Sevigny.*

Photos: Robert Damora

59

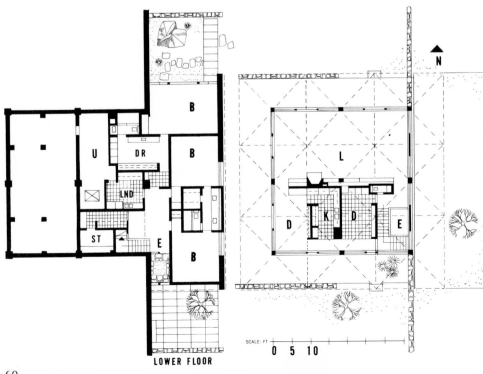

LOWER FLOOR

SCALE: FT   0 5 10

N

For all its drama, the house is designed for convenience and easy upkeep. The plan was devised by Franzen to simplify living for a family with only part-time commuting help. The house is replete with up-to-date equipment, and an abundance of built-in storage cabinets. Head-high storage units, finished in walnut or painted white, form the only separation of spaces in the upper living areas; thus the sense of space is increased, and the full impact of the roof structure is felt throughout the area. The lower level contains bedrooms for the children, flanking a compartmented bath; a master bedroom suite with a little court; and laundry, storage and utility rooms. The upper level is surrounded by broad decks, and contains a breakfast or hobby area in addition to the living, dining and kitchen areas. The master bedroom suite is designed with provision for a kitchenette, so that it may be used as a self-contained apartment. One of the children's rooms doubles as a guest room; each room has a sliding door for ventilation, and to serve as its own entrance from the outside.

Earl R. Flansburgh & Associates
Dover, Massachusetts   1966

The concept of developing the design of a house as a village-like complex has been used to singular advantage here to adapt a house to a dramatically rocky and forested site. From the top of the principal rock outcropping, it was possible to view the entire surrounding countryside to a distance of five miles in three directions, and 10 miles in the fourth. Thus, this was the spot on the 15-acre plot chosen as the house site. The obvious difficulties in planning for such a site, however, were turned into advantages by the architect. The necessity to fit the house around the rock projections led to a very functional, zoned unit plan which exactly fit the owners' requirements; and the entire house was designed to float visually above the rock, with the crisp, geometric lines of the structure contrasting with the sharp, irregular lines of the worn granite.

The architect remarks that ''one of the major problems of this project was to make the transition from the guest-parking level to the living room in an interesting fashion—a linear distance of approximately 100 feet and a total vertical rise and fall of about 25 feet. To accomplish this, the visitor climbs a stair rising along the northeast face of the rock, with varied exposures allowing the visitor to experience a full variety of views. Once inside the house, he is led past an indoor garden with a monitor overlooking yet another exposure.''

LYMAN RESIDENCE, Dover, Massachusetts. Owners: *Mr. and Mrs. Arthur T. Lyman, Jr.* Architects: *Earl R. Flansburgh & Associates.* Structural engineers: *Souza & True.* Heating and ventilating engineers: *Francis Associates.* Contractor: *Kurt Fuchs Co.* Landscape architect: Carol R. Johnson.

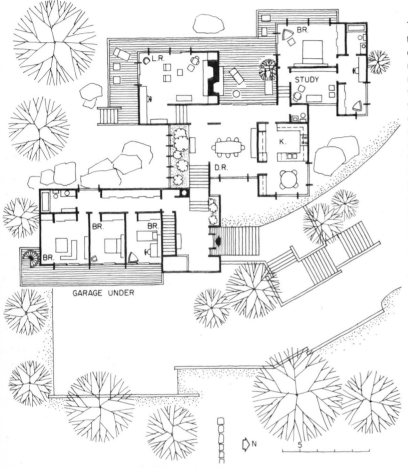

The somewhat loose organization of the plan has permitted a number of desirable zoning arrangements and room orientations in the Lyman residence. One of the paramount ones was the creation of a "children's wing," which allows the three children's bedrooms to be closed off when the children are away at school or have left home. A circular stair at the end of their balcony allows the children to enter their rooms directly from the outside. The master bedroom suite and the adjoining study are also isolated from the remainder of the house to allow the children to use the living room without disturbing the parents. This separation is achieved partially by a sheltered porch, built between the master bedroom and living room, and designed as an outdoor living-dining area protected from the frequent winds.

Since the Lyman family entertains frequently in the late afternoon and evening, the living room was oriented to look out to the south and west. The breakfast room, on the other hand, looks to the east and north to catch the morning sun at all times of the year. The "monitor" area was planned adjoining the dining room to allow extra space.

As can be noted in the plan, each major room in the Lyman house is provided with an adjoining outdoor deck. For the snowy months of winter, an indoor garden area is provided in the special "monitor" off the dining room, shown in the section and photograph at the far right.

Because of the family's varied interests, a generous amount of storage has been distributed throughout the house. Garage space for three cars is on the lower level.

The house is of simple span, wood frame construction on dark concrete foundations. The exterior siding is of rough, unplaned pine, with facing of smooth pine, and fins of plywood. The decks are stained pine; and the roof is tar and gravel.

The architect states that "the rough texture of the siding was designed to contrast with the smooth facia and fins. The dark concrete foundation was meant to emphasize the floating nature of the house over and around the rock. Although the house is a complicated series of planes, simple framing gave considerable economy in construction." The cost of the house was about $72,000, excluding lot.

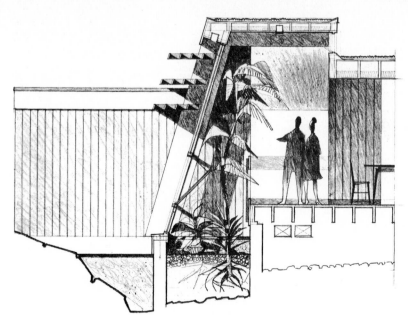

I.M.Pei & Associates
Washington, D.C.
1964

When Urban Renewal Administration Commissioner William Slayton and his family planned to return to the city after living in a suburban home, a search of the older, built-up neighborhoods of Washington turned up a bypassed, vacant lot in the Cleveland Park area. I. M. Pei's design for the property has produced a handsome, contemporary version of a town house with a walled-in front court. The lot measures 50 by 135 feet, and has a slight slope away from the street. This slope was used to advantage in creating a split-level scheme well suited to family life in the city. Great privacy was achieved, not only by the high wall of the front court, but by almost completely blank walls on the sides—which are quite close to existing houses. Inside, however, the feeling is one of great openness, with front and back walls of glass. The structure is brick bearing wall, topped by a triple, poured concrete vault. The interiors are brick and plaster.

SLAYTON RESIDENCE, Washington, D.C. Owners: *Mr. and Mrs. William M. Slayton.* Architects: *I.M. Pei & Associates—project manager: Kellogg Wong.* Engineers: *Severud-Elstad-Krueger Associates.* Landscape architect: *Ray V. Murphy.*

Photos: Joseph W. Molitor

The Slayton house gains a great sense of space and variety by good zoning and its split-level scheme. At the front, the house appears to be a single, high-ceilinged story. The main living areas and adjoining walled-in garden are on this side. Other rooms, each one bay wide, form a two-story section at the rear, left. A "service spine" is a buffer between. The spatial quality of the vaulted rooms is quite impressive. Mr. Slayton comments: "I remember clearly the day—when it was just becoming twilight—that I drove by the house when the forms for the vaulted roof had been removed. I walked through what is now the glass doors into this space, and for the first time realized what I. M. Pei had conceived. It was a tremendously moving and emotional experience; I shall never forget it." The vault over the stair is further dramatized by a skylight (across-page top).

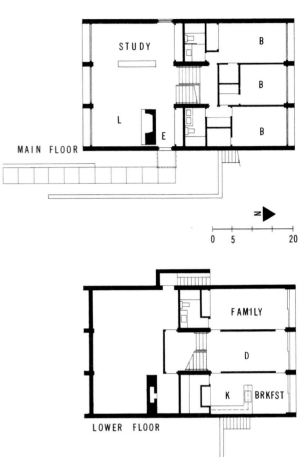

STUDY · B · B · B · L · E

MAIN FLOOR

N ▶

0   5   20

FAMILY · D · K · BRKFST

LOWER FLOOR

SECTION

"That one is for small talk."

3. INITIATIVES FOR MAKING LIFE

The romance with industrialization in house construction inevitably fostered, early on, an architectural concept of the house itself as a "machine for living," with maximum efficiency as its goal. Post-war era economic and social forces abetted the concept by making the cost and space for servants increasingly difficult to cope with—if, indeed, anyone could be found to do the menial work.

With household chores assumed largely by the owners, all eagerly sought ways in their new houses to speed up and lighten the added burdens. Architectural and planning "efficiency experts" had a field day measuring steps and arm-reach storage positions; counting items to scrub, dust or polish; and estimating heavy weights to shift. All was duly recorded, analyzed, published—and soon incorporated into new house plans.

The immediate architectural results were more compact kitchens and baths, more durable and easily maintained surfaces, labor saving devices, more and better organized storage, lighter furniture and less clutter and furbelows. Built-ins solved some of the problems, and manufacturers promptly revamped their products to help fulfill others of these near-universal goals.

As all these simplifications augmented the similar, and concurrent, architectural efforts to increase the sense of space, finding even more ways to improve facilities for servantless "modern living" gained momentum. Magazines flourished in transmitting these building ideas and time savers. The quest is enduring as socio-economics continue to change, and singles or small family units with a working wife tend to replace the big baby boom households of the 1950s. As the years advance, all this is reflected in the houses.

But the concern for easing and simplifying life didn't rest solely with "things." Rooms and spaces, and their uses and relationships were thoroughly scrutinized. Automobiles were shifted from their detached stables into garages or carports incorporated in the house, and given direct sheltered access

to a family entrance and to kitchen and storage areas. The kitchen itself was frequently moved from its more or less concealed location and placed at the front of the house for easier surveillance of the main entrance and street activity (for these purposes, it gradually replaced the front porch). Pass-throughs were introduced to ease kitchen to dining area service, or dining was re-placed in the kitchen. "Mud rooms" were formed at family entrances to minimize mess. Living rooms were pushed to the back of the house to take advantage of sequestered indoor-outdoor living spaces. Noisy activities were relegated to "rumpus rooms." With smaller, neater equipment, laundries were relocated to adjoin bedrooms and baths, where the washing was generated.

All in all, no traditional room relationship was left uncontested or unexplored, as the houses in this volume testify. So many of these changes have become firmly established themselves, now, that it is sometimes difficult to realize the care and thought that went into their implementation—of the countless bubble charts architects drew to examine new juxtapositions, of the air of innovation and publicity with which they were introduced. Some women's magazines held large nationwide conferences to discuss their readers' wants and needs, then devoted endless pages to presenting architectural solutions. Today, women's activist groups are holding similar meetings to urge new changes for now.

The experiments with open planning and room flexibility, as noted in a previous chapter, heralded other space relationships to add convenience—the open family-room–kitchen, the living-dining area, the guest room–study, are examples—and sought to provide quick-change potentials for special occasions and changing needs. Unit and sectional seating and storage were designed to facilitate the changes. But such flexibility did add work and create incongruities in some cases. Cartoonist Alan Dunn, among others, was quick to note and question them: "Keep the kids out of my open plan" and "Please leave

EASIER

so I can make the dining room," were among his benignly barbed captions.

Perhaps as a social goal, perhaps to mentally alleviate the potential friction, togetherness became a respected by-word and was put into practice by many in their multi-use spaces. Maybe long hours of communal TV-watching helped.

Others required some degree of personal privacy, and individual rooms (however small), zoning and sound control were provided for them—along with the bigger spaces for entertaining and family activities.

Technical improvements, compactness, lower costs in climate control (and its attendant condensation control), lighting, kitchen and bath equipment, even central vacuuming and sound systems, continued to add to ease and comfort. Utility companies sponsored and urged the "All Electric House" or the "All Gas House," often with lower utility rates and equipment give-aways if one complied. The recall of that not-so-long-ago era may be bittersweet with today's energy crunch, but at the time the promotion and cost-saving enticements did much to indelibly change our way of life and the shape of our houses. Such previous luxuries approached the norm, and others—especially swimming pools and (then unneeded) open fireplaces—abounded.

But efficiency, simplification and mechanization don't necessarily add up to a total panacea for easy, comfortable life. Some reaction, some re-instatement of pleasing inefficiency, was inevitable. For example, many are just happier in a big, rambling kitchen, regardless of its efficiency, and demand it; some enjoy skilled food chopping more than turning on "La Machine." And, all along, many (if not most) have delved in or collected some form of arts and crafts requiring proud display. Cosy, colorful clutter makes some more genuinely at ease, and though conscious of all those tenets of efficiency, they choose the added upkeep for added pleasure.

Yet the important thing is that the choices are—and have

been—there; the absolute "machine for living" has not been built. A close look at the houses of the near past, at the *Record Houses* represented in this volume, will reveal the outpouring of handsome, liveable variations that thoughtful architects have painstakingly designed for the individual preferences and comfort of the owners.

Edward Larrabee Barnes   1957
Mount Kisco, New York

A fresh, new use of a raised terrace, coupled with a sensitively designed open plan, marks this as a very distinguished house for a small family. The deft blend of casualness and formality in its design also make it unusually adaptable, for its size, to the inevitable variety of everyday and special family activities.

Although the idea of raising a house on a "platform" is hardly new (it has been associated with buildings in the Grand Manner, of course, all through history), the freshness lies in its use to such advantage for a small house. On a country hilltop site as this, it gives the house importance and expands the defined living area. It also minimizes the maintenance of sizeable grounds. Garden areas and lawns are confined to platform. The rest of the land needs only rough, occasional mowing. The entrance garden (photo right) is planned to look well winter and summer: myrtle and ivy are used as ground cover, with flowers peeking through in season.

BARNES RESIDENCE, Mount Kisco, New York. Architect: *Edward Larrabee Barnes*. Heating engineer: *Benjamin Spivak*. Landscape architect: *James Fanning*. Contractor: *August Nelson*.

The plan of the Edward Barnes house is basically conceived as one big room which combines terrace, living area, entrance hall, master bedroom and kitchen. Yet each individual area has its own importance and privacy. The bedroom doubles as a library, with the bed set back from living room view. A sliding door can close off the room.

The kitchen is treated as a major room, with full windows and careful detailing. It includes a pleasant dining area. The food preparation area is screened from the living room, and there is a sliding door. The dining table is moved to the living room for large parties. A convenient service entrance adjoins the kitchen and contains the laundry.

The main entrance hall is defined by a storage wall flanking the fireplace. The cabinets are fitted to store outdoor clothes, tools, linen, hi-fi equipment and games. As in the rest of the house, storage is well planned and handled in a neat, unobtrusive manner. The entire back wall of the house is of glass, shielded by trees and outside blinds.

Photos: Ben Schnall

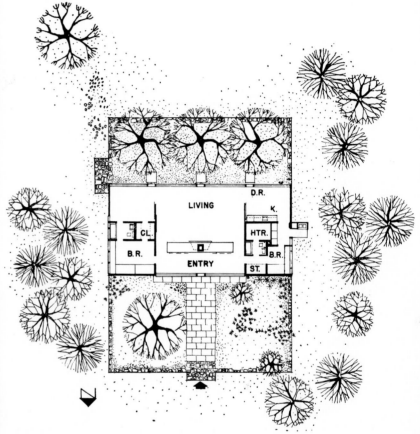

Jones & Emmons
Los Angeles, California
1956

Flexibility in plan is often a vital, necessary quality in today's smaller houses. During the course of the average family's lifetime, space and plan arrangement requirements can change considerably. In many houses, drastic changes in the plan are a near impossibility, and occupants must adjust to it as well as they can.

This house for Mr. and Mrs. A. Quincy Jones in Los Angeles, California, is specifically planned for such changes. Concrete slab floors, and metal columns and ceiling are permanent, but all walls are free-standing and movable. For temporary changes during the day, sliding and curtain partitions permit subdivision of areas into private rooms. All areas are multi-purpose.

The master bedroom doubles as an extension of the main living area, or as a library. The children's bedrooms form a large playroom. The kitchen is a family dining room, and part of the general living area. And the entire house can be opened wide to the outdoors.

One of the most unique features of the house is perhaps the unusual indoor-outdoor relationship created by bringing garden strips into the house through the entrance, and along the periphery of exterior walls.

JONES RESIDENCE, Los Angeles, California. Architects: *A. Quincy Jones and Frederick E. Emmons—associate architect: Emiel Becsky.* Contractor: *Morris Pynoos.*

Photos: Julius Shulman

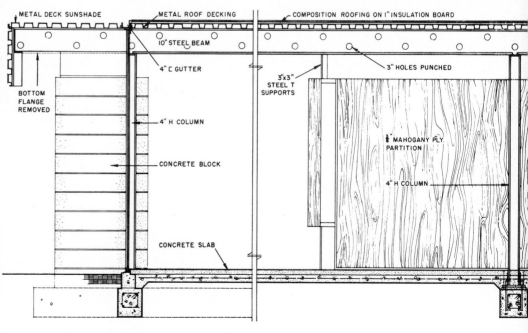

METAL DECK SUNSHADE — METAL ROOF DECKING — COMPOSITION ROOFING ON 1" INSULATION BOARD

10" STEEL BEAM

4" C GUTTER

3"x3" STEEL T SUPPORTS

3" HOLES PUNCHED

BOTTOM FLANGE REMOVED

4" H COLUMN

⅜ MAHOGANY PLY. PARTITION

CONCRETE BLOCK

4" H COLUMN

CONCRETE SLAB

The garden quality of the A. Quincy Jones house is clearly seen in these photographs. Beginning at the outside entry (above), the planting strips run through the living area (above right) and even into the master bedroom (below right). Cut-outs and skylights in the metal roof decking flood them with sun. Arrangement of kitchen equipment is unusual. Cooking units are built into cabinets and furniture (right); two range burners are in the family dining table, ovens are in an adjoining storage and serving cabinet. The bath-dressing area has a number of compartments, each accessible from all bedrooms.

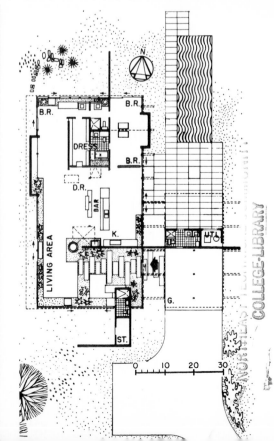

Willis N. Mills, Jr.
Van Hornesville, New York
1967

Photos: Milton Weinstock

Unity and diversity in a large country house are achieved through individual expression of separate functions—bound together by uniformity of roof pitch, consistent use of materials and balance of the forms themselves.

The architect was faced with the problem of designing a spacious house capable of accommodating large family gatherings from time to time, but one not so grand as to feel empty or overpowering for the day-to-day life of a family of four. While a great deal of space was needed, the owners were anxious to avoid anything approaching "manor house" proportions and wanted a home which would fit in with the character of the local farming community.

Architect Mills' solution places bedrooms and living areas in distinct wings —separated by a flat-roofed link building containing playroom and breakfast room—with a detached guesthouse (right in photo above and plot plan) capable of accommodating two family groups

in separate two-bedroom units. Cedar shingle roofs and charcoal gray redwood siding, contained within a frame of white skirt, fascia and cornerboards—described by the architect as "a common barn-building vernacular"—were deliberately chosen to harmonize with the older buildings in the neighborhood. But the brilliant red front door provides a light-hearted expression of the architect's personality. The over-all massing of the buildings gives the impression of a farm complex that is comfortably at home in the countryside.

The site commands a long view to the east overlooking the Mohawk valley, and two other pleasant but less dramatic views. The three-way orientation of the living areas makes the most of all views.

CASE RESIDENCE, Van Hornesville, New York. Owners: *Mr. and Mrs. James H. Case III.* Architect: *Willis N. Mills, Jr.* Mechanical engineer: *John Moran.* Contractor: *Marion H. Baker.*

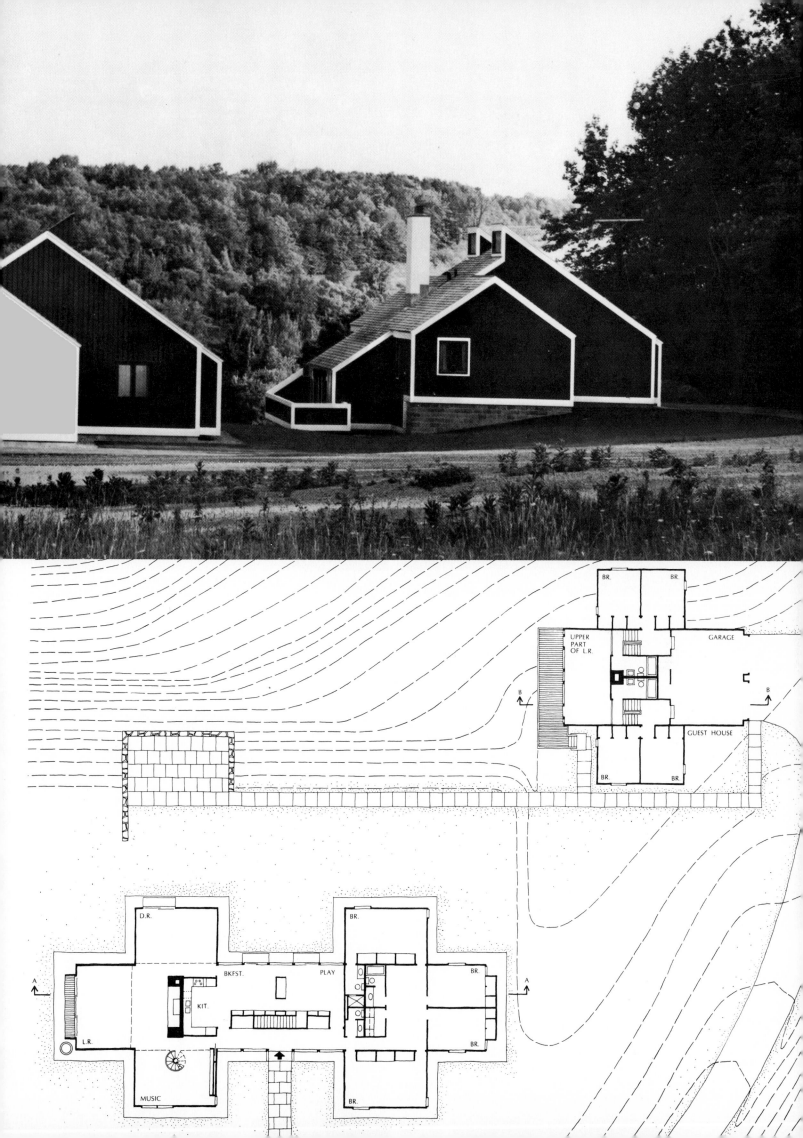

UPPER PART OF L.R.

GARAGE

BR.

BR.

BR.

BR.

GUEST HOUSE

B

B

D.R.

BR.

BKFST.

PLAY

KIT.

BR.

BR.

A

A

L.R.

MUSIC

BR.

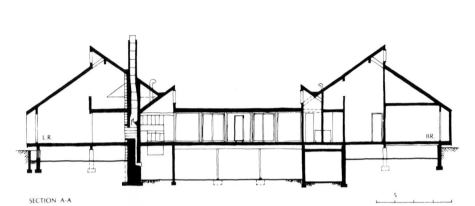

SECTION A-A

5

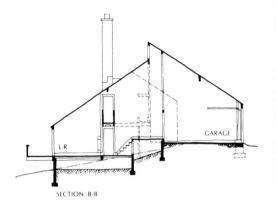

SECTION B-B

Milton Weinstock

Milton Weinstock

High, sloping ceilings dramatize the main living areas of the Case house, while the use of balconies, beams and unusual stairways fully exploits the spatial potential of a rather rambling fragmented plan. However, as the architect says, "the complexity of these diverse elements is held together by a constant series of materials" throughout both the main house (photos and section left) and the guesthouse (right). All walls are rough sand-finish plaster, sloping ceilings are one-inch by 4-inch redwood boards, and the flat ceilings are hard white plaster. Redwood framing for windows and doors is balanced by the redwood mantle over the fireplace. Floors in the living areas are dark-stained oak strip, while vinyl cork tile is used in kitchen, bathrooms and playroom. A five-zoned oil-fired warm-air heating system gives a comfortable environment throughout the house.

The guesthouse makes use of a change of grade to place the living room and kitchen on a lower level and the two sets of bedrooms above, each with its own stairway, entrance hall and bathroom. The garage is located in back of the same building.

Commenting on how the house has reacted to use and time, the architect says that he has been pleased with "the way it absorbs large groups on occasions without seeming rattlingly empty the rest of the time. The choice of solid natural materials used in a rather elemental way seems to have worn well and contributed to the character of the neighborhood."

© Ezra Stoller Associates

Hugh Newell Jacobsen
Eastern Shore, Maryland

1971

In size and scale and form and rambling shape, this house on the shores of Chesapeake Bay is reminiscent of the elegant manor houses of Maryland's Eastern Shore. But these characteristics give way under architect Hugh Jacobsen's hand to a thoroughly contemporary house that is thoughtfully and functionally zoned; dramatic (indeed sometimes spectacular) but always human in scale; full of pleasant surprises; and—very consciously—starkly contrasted against its site.

Jacobsen's essential scheme, from which everything else follows, was to divide the house into four elements, each with its own steeply pitched roof. As the plan shows, each element is a separate zone—garage/utility, kitchen/dining, entry/living room, and bedroom/library—so positioned that every room overlooks the view, circulation is sensible and straightforward, and the handsome stone-paved entry court is formed.

The house is built of white stucco over block, with a black asphalt shingle roof set off by the parapets that sharply define the edges of each element against the sky. All of the glass—both fixed and operative—is tinted and tempered plate. Interior finishes are drywall on walls and ceiling, floors are oak except in the kitchen.

Jacobsen's attention to detail is evident everywhere: in the slit windows that permit surprise views from many rooms; in the slit skylights which give unexpected glimpses of the sky and contribute to an ever-changing quality of light; in the slender detailing of the screen porch and window framing; in the strongly expressed rain gutters with anchor chain "down-spouts." Other examples: in the bedroom wing, pockets in the walls contain a sliding glass panel, a screen panel, and a teak louvered panel for privacy and light control.

And everywhere, inside and out, there is an absence of casings or moldings or bases or trim—an absence of detail which is the best but always the most difficult kind of detailing.

Architect: Hugh Newell Jacobsen. *Location:* Eastern Shore, Maryland. *Structural engineer:* James Madison Cutts. *Mechanical engineer:* Alexander Blumenthal. *Contractor:* Ships Point Construction Company.

Robert C. Lautman photos

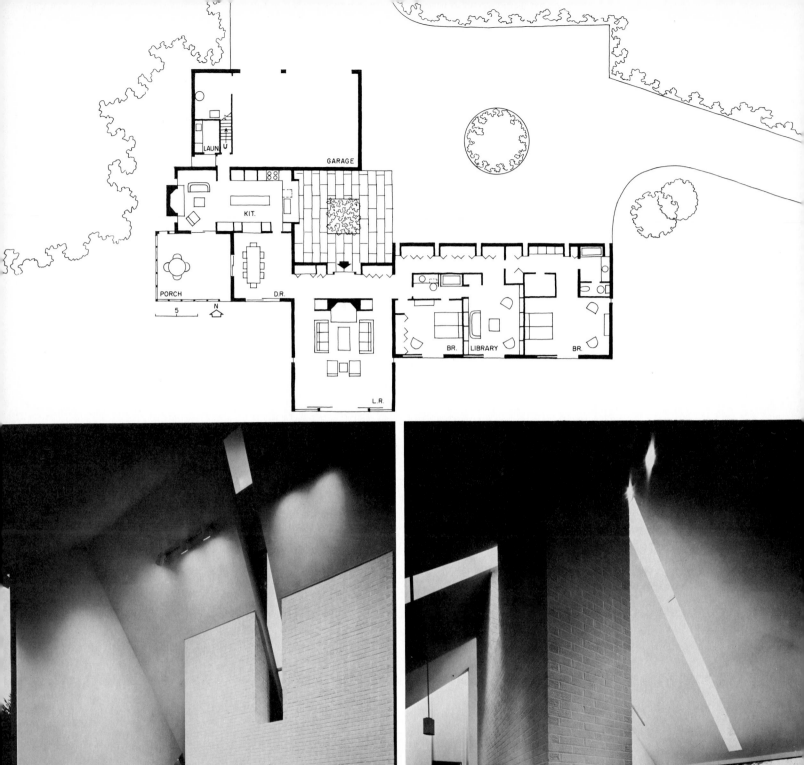

Architect Jacobsen's careful detailing is evident throughout the interiors. Ceilings follow the form of the roof, are slit by skylights. The fireplace wall separates living room from entry (above). The kitchen (opposite) has its own seating area in front of the dramatic glass-framed fireplace.

Don Hisaka & Associates
Northern Ohio
1976

When the architect and owners first explored the possibilities for this densely-wooded, 150-acre site, a "tree-house" with expansive outdoor decks seemed a reasonable starting point for conceptual design. As the functional requirements became clearer and more precisely defined, the tree house notion was modified to a more conventional elevated platform structure, but the broad areas of deck remained and a sense of living among the trees persisted as an important design theme.

The primary spaces in the house are grouped into two wings—one for parents, one for offspring—and in each case, vertical zoning places sleeping areas above living areas (see plans, opposite page). The two wings are linked by a short, glass-enclosed bridge. Openings, as well as decks, are oriented toward handsome views of three man-made lakes that change their aspect both by time of day and season. A fourth lake lies out of sight from the house a quarter mile to the west. The rest of the property is heavily wooded, giving the house an unusual degree of isolation and a special sense of its own privacy.

The enrichment of the simple cube forms by careful, knife-edged additions and subtractions, the consistency of the white-painted plywood exterior and the detachment of the whole mass from the earth plane combine to make this house stand apart from its natural surroundings—not in conflict with them, but in sharply focused contrast.

PRIVATE RESIDENCE, Ohio. Architects: *Don Hisaka & Associates—project architect: George Saire.* Structural engineers: *Gensert-Peller Associates.* Mechanical engineers: *George Evans & Associates.* Electrical engineers: *Lombardi & Associates.* Contractor: *Buell Davidson.*

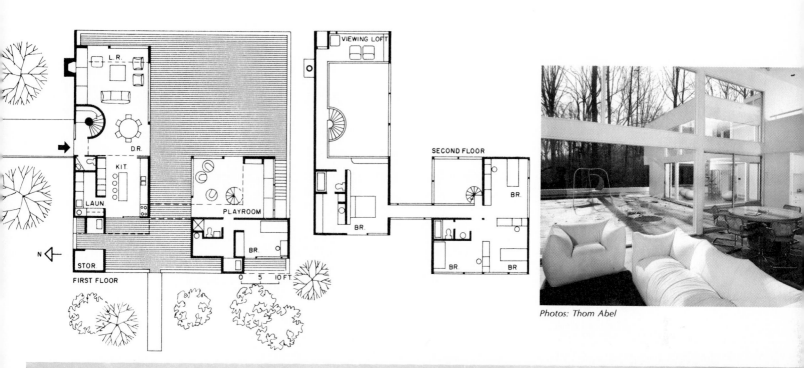

FIRST FLOOR

L.R. DR. KIT. LAUN. STOR. PLAYROOM BR.

N

0 5 10 FT

VIEWING LOFT SECOND FLOOR BR. BR. BR. BR.

Photos: Thom Abel

1967

The Stillman house demonstrates the effectiveness of a simple uncluttered architectural form when careful detailing, concern for light and shade and sensitive handling of materials combine to establish a harmonious relationship with a pleasant, rural site.

The plan is straightforward, functional and relaxed with a central living-dining area flanked at one end by the children's- and guest-bedroom wing, and on the other by the master bedroom suite—separated by its bathroom from the utility and darkroom area.

Approaching the house between fieldstone walls and up some steps, you pass through a walled-in, gravelled courtyard to enter the glass-fronted living room. The fieldstone and stucco exterior walls are carried through into the interior, where the stone base has been extended to provide attractive, casual seating, or display ledges for ornaments, sculpture or plants. The stone skirting and the rough, brick floors are offset by the white stucco walls, which form a quiet background for an interesting art collection. At the back of the house, a vegetable garden leads through to the site of a projected swimming pool farther up the hill and a Calder mobile sculpture strategically placed on the crown of the slope. The courtyard in front makes a pleasant outdoor room, which can be used for summer dining and entertaining, for the display of sculpture, or simply sitting quietly in the shade.

The natural slope of the site places the main entrance a full story above grade. Changes in level are articulated by the variation in the height of the fieldstone base, by the steps leading up to the courtyard and more steps leading down into the living room from the entry area.

STILLMAN RESIDENCE, Litchfield, Connecticut. Owners: *Mr. and Mrs. Rufus C. Stillman.* Architects: *Marcel Breuer and Herbert Beckhard.* Contractors: *Hirsch Brothers.*

Photos: Joseph W. Molitor

Breuer & Beckhard
Litchfield, Connecticut

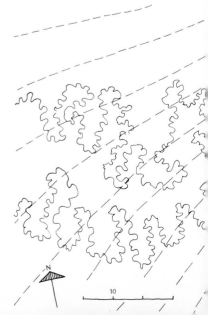

Classic modern furniture, much of it designed by Breuer himself, adds to the restrained elegance of the interiors. The fireplaces are supported on the projecting stone base walls and in two of the bedrooms have convenient log-stacking cubbyholes beneath the hearth. The kitchen and dining areas are in effect a single room and no attempt has been made to conceal any of the functions of cooking and meal preparation. This is part of the informal concept of the house which specifically fits the owners' requirements. In all rooms, bold paintings exploit white walls.

Mayers & Schiff & Associates
Long Island, New York

1980 This complex and carefully-studied house rises up from a relatively flat site to give its occupants controlled views of field and pine woods to the north and west, and a superb, panoramic view of dunes and ocean to the south. It is a large house for a large family, with guest functions isolated in an independent, two-story structure to the north.

Two devices have been used to unify the plan. Both are unusual. The first is a long exterior wall that separates two side-by-side circulation routes—one the public approach, the other a private, glass-enclosed link between the main house

and the guest quarters. A second unifying device is a pair of structural cores, one in the guest quarters, one in the main house. The cores are necessary as wind-bracing elements because the exterior walls are so fully opened that they no longer act as diaphragms. These cores, enclosing minor spaces, run the full length of each volume and express themselves on the elevations as white, stucco-clad projections that stand in stark contrast to the cedar used to clad the rest of the frame. Inside, the identity of the cores is maintained by lowered ceilings and the use of white-painted gypsum board and white tile,

materials and colors that are used nowhere else.

Major spaces take shape around these cores. The heart of the house is a double-height living room joined by a dining room and kitchen that together make a strong linear volume that is open to views on three sides. The master bedroom, over the dining space, opens to a private deck that overlooks the Atlantic.

The site has been as thoughtfully developed as the house. The pine groves were thickened with new planting, and a lawn seeded on the east side of the house. In a sequestered hollow between

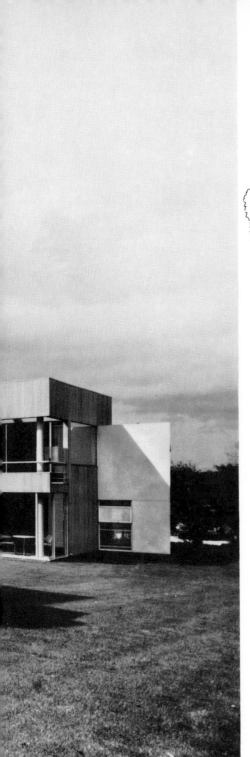

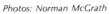

GUEST HOUSE & GARAGE

POOL

10

N

Photos: Norman McGrath

the house and the line of primary dunes, the architects have developed a gracious swimming pool and surrounding deck. The pool can be reached by guests through a passage under the house.

PRIVATE RESIDENCE, Long Island, New York. Architects: *Mayers & Schiff & Associates—project architect: Peter Wheelwright.* Structural engineers: Robert Silman. Mechanical engineers: *Michael Ambrosino.* Electrical engineers: *Robert Freudenberg.* Landscape architects: *Zion & Breen/Quennel Rothschild.* Contractor: *Caramagna & Murphy, Inc.*

Much of its delight derives from the concern for detail that has been bestowed so generously on this house by its designers. This high level of detail is visible in every photograph. The range of finish materials includes buff-colored floor tile, cedar boards on walls and ceilings, aluminum and steel sash, double glazing in all openings.

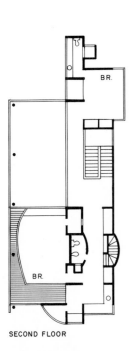

SECOND FLOOR

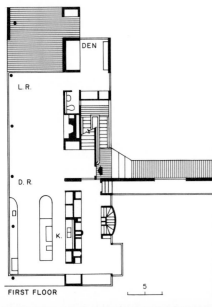

FIRST FLOOR

BR.

BR.

DEN

L.R.

D.R.

K.

5

Eliot Noyes
New Canaan, Connecticut

1957

The dramatic two-zone plan of this house separates formal and informal living areas by means of a central courtyard flanked on both sides by parallel wings. A rugged stone wall merges artfully with the heavily wooded landscape which surrounds the house, and yet is a forceful enough barrier to yield a secure sense of well-defined containment.

The bedroom area and living area are in separate wings. Covered walks at either end of the courtyard connect them. Entrance to either must be gained by traveling outside, along the walks. Walks could be glass-enclosed, though the sun and the heat which radiates from the house keep them free of snow—even during Connecticut winters.

The stone wall which closes in the garden (and house) at opposite ends is divided by massive wood doors which slide open to create dual gates to the garden. Closed, the doors offer protection against storms. The garden, which in effect becomes a room in the house, is well cultivated to contrast with rough surrounding landscape.

NOYES RESIDENCE, New Canaan, Connecticut. Architect: *Eliot Noyes.* Lighting Consultant: *Richard Kelly.* Contractor: *Borglum and Meed, Inc.*

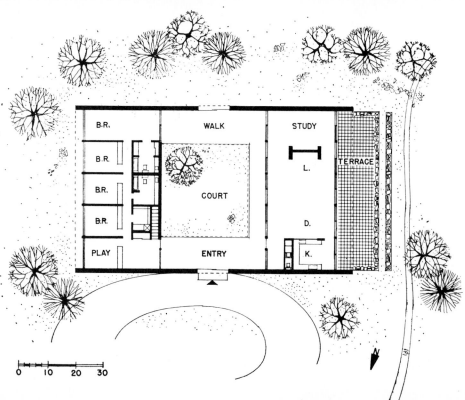

The plan of the Eliot Noyes house puts five bedrooms, baths, snackbar, laundry, storage, and sitting room areas along one wing. Four of the bedrooms face the Connecticut woods. The master bedroom spans the width of the wing, yielding a view of both woods and courtyard. The sitting room doubles as a playroom for the children and a family TV room. A snackbar equipped with combination refrigerator and range serves for early-morning coffee and late evening snacks. The other wing is composed of kitchen, dining area, living room and study. The kitchen is a compact horseshoe shape with pass-through to dining area. Living and dining areas are together, separated only by placement of furniture. Focal point in the living room is a stone-and-plaster fireplace which screens study. Floors are bluestone, walls are glass. Study is furnished with long table, bookshelves. Skylights in the study, which doubles as working area or extension of living room, provide additional natural lighting.

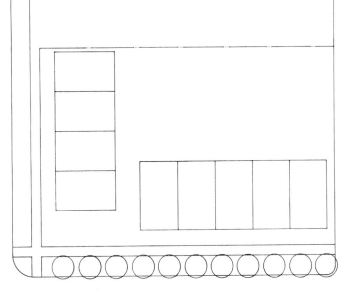

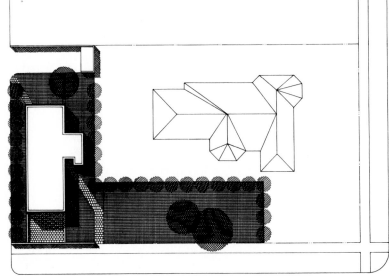

Booth & Nagel
Chicago, Illinois
1970

This elegant, extremely civilized house solves a number of the problems of space, privacy and views which confront anyone planning for a rapidly changing urban environment. The site was gerrymandered from the rear yard of an old residence, in a Chicago neighborhood that is beginning to be rebuilt with high density residential units.

To give a sense of openness, yet control the views, architects Booth & Nagle have designed all window openings so that little is seen of the surrounding buildings from inside the house—only trees, sky and the owners' little yard and terrace. Though the use of windows is fairly minimal, their effectiveness is intensified by running them from floor to ceiling in the two-story living room and in the three-story stairwell. A see-through, "endless vista" effect is created for the main living spaces by matching the

SECOND FLOOR

RECREATION

KIT.

D.R.

UPPER PART
OF L.R.

FIRST FLOOR

BR.

STUDY

L.R.

N

5

GROUND FLOOR

Phillip A. Turner photos

The interior furnishings were also planned by the architects, and are as spare, tidy and elegant as the house itself. Walls and ceilings are painted gypsum board, and all trim is carefully and simply detailed in oak. Except for the entry and kitchen (quarry tile) and the baths (unglazed ceramic tile), all floors are also oak. Hardware is brushed chrome and registers are brushed aluminum. Strong color accents are provided by paintings.

On the total concept, the architects comment, "this house is really thought by us to be a large scale structurist sculpture, unified by concern with only essentials: form, space, light, texture and color."

front windows with similar ones at the back, and creating (with the doors open) a five-foot-wide, open horizontal space running through the two lower levels; and on the opposite side of the house, there is a similar three-foot-wide space running through the dining level. The dining area itself is treated as a balcony to share in the two-story living space, and to create a fireplace nook below.

The trim, simple forms of the exterior are the direct expression of the interior plan: living spaces in the larger block, vertical circulation in the smaller.

The house is wood-framed on a concrete foundation, and clad in a sort of gray-brown brick. All details and trim have been carefully minimized and simplified, so that the design relies on the well related proportions of the solids created by the walls and the window voids.

BARGLOW RESIDENCE, Chicago, Illinois. Owners: *Dr. and Mrs. Peter Barglow.* Architects: *Laurence Booth and James Nagle of Booth & Nagle.* Interior design: *Booth & Nagle.* Contractor: *R. H. Roberts Construction Co.*

"Hey, what's going on up there!"

4. THE THRUSTS OF

Today, in coping with ever more precious resources of all kinds, and especially with the imminent perils of energy shortages, ecological concerns and constantly mounting inflation, it has become somewhat fashionable to condemn contemporary houses as profligate in all areas.

With a few, rare exceptions, the converse has been true. Since World War II, there has been great architectural concentration and effort spent on designing houses that would truly conserve—and wisely use—nature, energy resources, money and, often, existing structures. In fact, these very factors, along with the experiments in space, structure and comfort, have made houses the vigorous laboratory of design they have been. Priorities may have altered through the years, but the care has remained.

Of prime concern has always been the nature of the site itself, and how the house would relate to it—whether by contrast or blend. Before any actual design started, the land was carefully surveyed for all natural features—trees, grade changes, dunes, rock outcroppings, waterways, whatever there might be—that should be preserved and enjoyed on the actual building site; and note was made of the environs, the neighborhood, and the scenic distance (if any). In a good house, these all became closely integrated into its design, planning and orientation as invaluable assets; many less expensive, bypassed and "unbuildable" sites, from ravines to cliffs, provided dramatic design challenges and successes. Final landscaping of the sites tended to augment the natural features. Some architects, such as Don Metz in New Hampshire and William Morgan in Florida, carried this integration of house and site even further—setting a house, earth covered, directly into a hillside; or surrounding a house, dune-like, with earth berms.

Little of all this, obviously, is to be found in a bulldozed tract development. Nor is it in areas of little immediate topological interest or in areas of high density: in these situations,

architects have often created internal "environments" for their houses via glazed courts or even greenhouses, and created fairly blank facades towards any bleary outlook.

Much experimenting has been recurrent, also, in exploring ways in planning and orienting a house to best encourage—or fend off as the case may be—the natural elements. The natural energies of climate, of sun, wind, rain, snow, have all been studied for their beneficial or harmful effects on houses and their livability. The hermetically-sealed, totally air-conditioned house has been a rarity—even at the height of the era of energy plentifulness and low cost.

In the 1950s, planned sun penetration into a new house was usually elaborately researched and plotted, and a variety of sun control devices (overhangs, sun screens, blinds, shutters, "eyebrows," baffles, grilles—some fixed, some movable) were used to assure deep sun penetration of spaces in winter, a minimum in summer. The effects of glare were counteracted. The sizes of openings, positions of blank walls, and amount of insulation were studied and manipulated to augment benefits and protection.

Air currents and winds received equal attention. Rendered sections of the houses were drawn, both for study and to clearly demonstrate the advantages of planned cross ventilation and sun control to the owners. This study often gave the houses of that era a distinctive look, which varied with region and climate, as had earlier houses. Marcel Breuer's houses, for example, built in the Northeast during that period had "eyebrows" as a fairly constant signature. Other houses in more tropical areas sometimes had entire facades of adjustable louvers to assure control of sun, rain and breezes. In hurricane- or storm-prone areas, sliding barn-like doors or big hinged panels were often employed to add extra wind and rain security (and sometimes for protection against vandals when the house was vacant).

The emerging availability of stronger, insulating double-

CONSERVATION

glazed units and tinted glass for windows or walls obviated some of the protective measures that had been developed—but at a price. For a period, there was a perceptible move toward making any mechanism as invisible as possible, with heating by radiant floors or ceilings or baseboards—even by electric strips in the windows; and lighting turned toward such devices as indirect coves, luminous ceilings, and concealed pin-spots—but again at a price, in efficiency and money.

This was followed by a period of letting it all show (sometimes even the plumbing), which was possibly more an economic reaction than an esthetic one. As we all know, the economics were then ramified as fuel costs surged and supplies ebbed.

The popularity of the ever-present fireplaces or metal stoves bounded; and some older ideas and devices for solar heating (which had earlier been set aside as not entirely practical or economical) were resurrected and improved upon, first for hot water heating; then as solar heat collection and storage equipment improved even more, for heating the house. To these were added the—also resurrected—"passive" sun control methods and devices whose use had slowly waned through the years. For the most part, the results to date of these cumulative energy-saving methods continue to exhibit a decided "let it all show" appearance, but design experiments and refinements will certainly lead to a host of tidier, new regional looks before long.

The conservation attitude of making the best use of what is there, of making more from less, has been a continuing thread through the last quarter century. Its materializations have ranged from using some of the newest ways to lower costs (as in Henri Gueron's elegant little East Hampton house, built for only $15,000 as late as 1972), to an ever-mounting passion for converting often improbable indigenous structures into modern houses—starting with barns in the 1950s, and ranging through carriage houses, silos and jerry-built older houses, to a Boston auto repair shop by Paul Rudolph. The urge to save has produced many interesting results.

Moore Grover Harper

Eastern Shore Maryland

1978

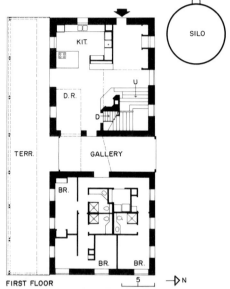

SILO

KIT.

D.R.

U

D

TERR.

GALLERY

BR.

BR. BR.

FIRST FLOOR   5   →N

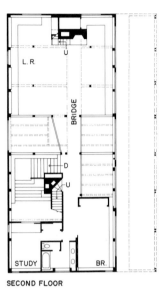

L.R.

U

BRIDGE

D

U

STUDY

BR.

SECOND FLOOR

The owners of this old barn placed some unusual constraints on the architects they commissioned to convert it to a second home. Certain of the constraints, in addition, seemed in a sense to conflict. The owners wanted the renovation to be energy-efficient, for instance, but they also wanted the original siding and roofing to be retained and remain visible from within. They wanted the first-floor structure of stone walls (circa 1850) and hand-hewn timbers to be celebrated, but they also wanted the barn highly receptive to the sun.

To accomplish these priorities, the architects begn by building new exterior walls, fastening them by means of ledger strips to the old plates. New rough siding was also applied and left to weather. Because the old rafters could not support another layer of roofing, the architects nailed 2x6s through the existing metal roof into the rafters creating a "T" section that would support new horizontal members and a new metal roof. The cavity this created was filled with insulation.

Along its south wall, the old barn had been built with an integral shed. But the shed cut off long views to the Choptank River as well as winter sunlight, so the architects stripped it of its siding, removed sections of its roof and in this manner created a trellised structure (photo right) that adds enormously to the character of the renovation.

Five solar collectors on the south-facing section of the roof provide domestic hot water, while a conventional oil burner is used for space heating. When the house is unoccupied, the two systems are set in tandem and the thermostat set way down.

"We worked hard," says Mark Simon, "to retain and even enhance the rough-hewn character and yawning openness that makes this building a barn, while at the same time giving attention to special places where the inhabitants live and play."

A marvelous renovation.

BARN RENOVATION, Maryland. Architects: *Moore Grover Harper—project architects: Charles Moore, Mark Simon.* Structural engineer: *Ronald Schaeffer.* Interiors: *Samuel Marrow.* Landscape architect: *Lester Collins.* Contractor: *LGR, Inc.*

Photos: Norman McGrath

The major spaces are distributed over three levels or partial levels. The entry is on the west wall and leads to a small vestibule. From here, the view leads to a broad staircase that passes behind a stucco-covered chimney up to the second-floor living room. A second flight of steps leads to the third floor. As the photos eloquently show, all the major spaces are anticipated through a tantalizing fretwork of beams, posts and braces. Wherever possible, the architects have retained details and hardware from the earlier era—the wood bolt on the door (previous page) being a fine example.

Don Metz
Lyme, New Hampshire
1974

On property he already owned in Lyme, New Hampshire, designer Don Metz built this sod-roofed house for sale. "I was bothered," says Metz, who holds a Masters degree in architecture from Yale, "by the prospect of anything other than the low-profile, 'anti-building' solution I knew the site demanded, so I borrowed and built on spec. The present owners—Mr. and Mrs. Oliver Winston were interested before it was completed, made a few minor changes, and that was that."

The finished house is built into a mountainside and embraces a panoramic, 50-mile view to the south. Metz has drawn the earth back down over the roof to a depth of 16 inches. Wildflowers and grasses have already taken root and a stand of nearby maples is slowly spreading to the rooftop. Its designer hopes the house will gradually disappear among the things that grow around it.

Metz reports that in winter solar gain is sufficient on sunny days to keep the temperatures in the house up to 70°F while outside temperatures are as low as zero. In summer, when the thermal process is reversed, the insulating mantle of earth keeps the house pleasantly cool.

The projections through the sod roof are functional and, though some readers may feel that they compromise the purity of the design parti, it is hard to see how to do without light scoops or roof vents in a plan with such a long "blind" perimeter. As constructed, the dining area (photo upper right) is suffused with natural light and free of unwelcome glare. The living room opens south across a terrace and small pool to a broad vista of mountain and valley.

Exterior walls are concrete block spanned on 18-inch centers by 6- by 10-in. pine beams. Floors are oak strips nailed over sleepers. The roof is built-up (see detail, opposite page) and finished with a parapet of vertical boards.

WINSTON HOUSE, Lyme, New Hampshire, Designer and contractor: *Don Metz*. Structural engineers: *Spiegel & Zamecnik, Inc.* Landscape architect: *Dan Kiley*. Built-ins: *William Porter, Inc.*

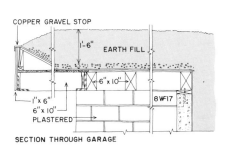

COPPER GRAVEL STOP

EARTH FILL

1'-6"

6" x 10"

1" x 6"
6" x 10"
PLASTERED

8 WF17

SECTION THROUGH GARAGE

GARAGE

ST.

STUDY D.R. K

BR. MUSIC L.R. BR.

N

5

Robert Perron photos

Hobart D. Wagener
Boulder, Colorado
1967

This house, planned around an interior garden covered by a 24-foot-square skylight, is designed to compensate for Colorado's arid climate. The result is the creation of a special environment "where vines rather than walls are used to separate living areas," as the architect describes it. The rapid rate of plant growth in the garden was a surprise: within a year, many kinds of ferns and evergreens, grapefruit, lemon and banana trees were thriving, and poinsettias were nine feet tall.

In a further effort to counteract the semibarren countryside, there are several enclosed exterior spaces. The fencing around the greater part of the property is of cedar plywood with redwood battens, to match the exterior wood surface of the house and make it an integral part of the front façade.

The main living, kitchen and bedroom areas are disposed around the garden on the ground floor, but a balcony over the kitchen and bedroom areas provides two additional bedrooms, a bathroom and a study for the two teen-age children. A partial basement is included beneath the kitchen-dining room area.

The closed-in front or street facade is in sharp contrast to the back of the house where glass walls open to a view of an adjacent golf course to the south and west, with the Rocky Mountains in the background. The deep, sheltering roof provides physical and psychological protection in a climate of extremes.

Architect and owner: Hobart D. Wagener. *Location:* Boulder, Colorado. *Structural engineer:* W. B. Johnson; *Contractor:* R. C. Grayson Construction Company.

Norman McGrath photos

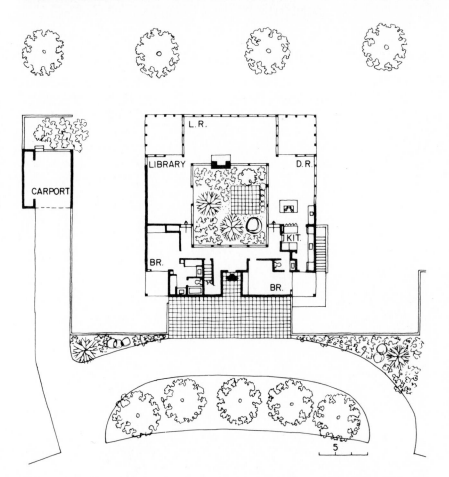

The roof structure is as dramatic a feature of the interior of the house as it is of the exterior. The simple, symmetrical composition of laminated wood beams and cedar decking is complemented by the wire-glass skylight area and the glass walls on the southern and western exposures.

The kitchen is divided into two areas, which can be separated by means of an oak folding door. In this way, the messy area can be closed off during meal-times, leaving the diners with a view of the rather attractive free-standing range and, as Hobart Wagener puts it, "the visually interesting part of food preparation."

The garden, which naturally enough is the main focus of the living areas, has its own central focus in the form of a brick island which makes an excellent base for sculpture, pottery or any kind of garden feature. A stone slab path leads through the garden to the island.

Furnishings are deliberately simple and elegant to avoid any conflict with the strongly articulated structure and plan of the building.

Gas-fired, forced-air heating and refrigerated cooling make for a comfortable environment at all seasons of the year.

Alfred N. Beadle
Phoenix, Arizona
1965

An asset was made of a difficult site problem in this trim house. The lot was chosen because of its desirable location and its undulating grades. However, it is a natural "wash" which carries off seasonal run-off water from the neighboring hills. To cope with it, the architect simply left the site undisturbed as a natural, pristine rock garden, raised the house on steel stilts, and enjoys the periodic streams running through. The entrance drive and pool terraces were built up a bit, with block retaining walls, so they would not flood during run-off times.

Raising the house itself gave an added bonus in gaining elevation to take advantage of a nice view to the south.

The design of the house contrasts a rather sophisticated, hard-edged structure with the natural rocky environment. It is totally contained in an exposed, modular steel frame with bays measuring 12 feet 4 inches by 14 feet 4 inches. The bays are used open or closed as the plan warranted, for rooms, terraces and planting areas. Enclosing walls are sliding glass doors or panels surfaced with cement plaster.

Rooms or terraces were planned to exactly fit a one or two bay space. The extensive use of glass walls and integrated outdoor spaces visually enlarges all the living areas in the house. Two combination heating and air conditioning systems (one three-ton, one five-ton) join with sensible zoning in the plan to provide a very liveable house.

BEADLE RESIDENCE, Phoenix, Arizona. Architect: *Alfred N. Beadle, Dailey Associates.* Contractor: *Len Pritchard.*

Jerry Duchscherer photos

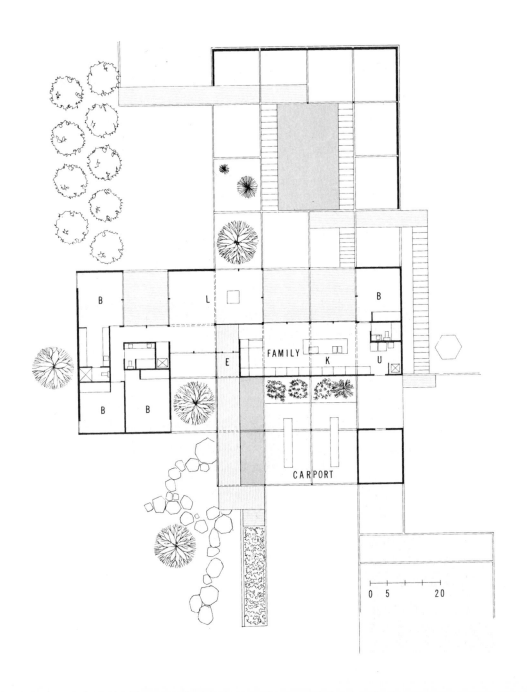

In his own house, Alfred Beadle used the regular, disciplined bay spacing as a "design motif" throughout the raised or built-up areas of house and grounds: the same module is used for dimension of planting beds, drive and the like. In these areas, planting is carefully controlled to contrast with the natural site—a device which considerably reduces the maintenance required for the grounds. It would be possible, if desired at a later date, to enclose some of the open deck areas in the house to enlarge some of the existing spaces, or to add new ones. As built, the house has 2400 square feet of interior space, and 4800 square feet of roofed space; quite a bit of luxury was included for a construction cost of approximately $37,000, excluding lot and landscaping.

The steel structure supports wood joists topped by plywood sheathing for floors and roof. The surfacing for the roof is a 4-ply built-up one; carpeting is used on the floors of most living areas. Four-inch batt insulation is installed in floors and ceilings as a thermal barrier.

All the interiors are finished with painted gypsum board, except the big family-room–kitchen, which is surfaced with walnut. The baths are all interior ones, daylighted by domed plastic skylights. The utilities of the house are ranged along the central bays to form a sort of extended "service spine." In addition to the generous storage provided in each room (including a good-sized dressing room for the master bedroom), there is a commodious storage "house" flanking the garage.

Wade Swicord photos

Dwight E. Holmes
Tampa, Florida
1972

Architect Dwight Holmes' house on Tampa Bay seems very much at home in what he calls "a near perfect example of semi-tropical environment: moderate temperatures, bright sun, generous rainfall and daily breezes off the Bay and Gulf." Placed well back from the street on a long and narrow lot, the house looks east across the open bay. Largely solid side walls of unfinished concrete block screen the house from uncertain future development on adjoining properties. The end elevations, however, are completely transparent. Four-panel sliding aluminum window walls stacked three high (right) form those facades. To control sun and to provide protection from tropical storms, a system of adjustable redwood louvers has been provided. The louvers have a shadow texture whose scale is adequately proportioned to the masonry planes. Within the severe rectangular volume, Holmes has created an appropriate openness by placing the dining and master bedroom platforms on the second and third floors at opposite ends of the plan, permitting two-story spaces for both living and dining rooms. The central utility core is designed to minimize interruptions of ventilation flow. Including central air conditioning for periods of intense heat and humidity, the house and a small studio behind it of similar construction cost $28,000.

Architect and owner: DWIGHT E. HOLMES. *Location:* Tampa, Florida. *Contractor:* Ranon and Jimenez.

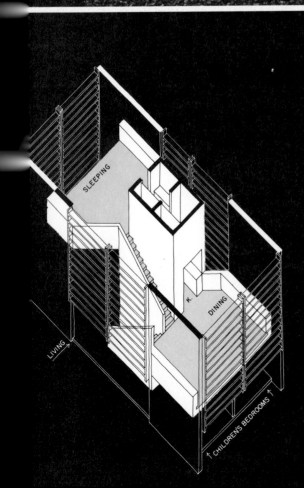

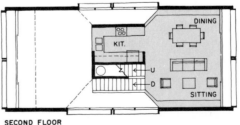

SLEEPING

THIRD FLOOR

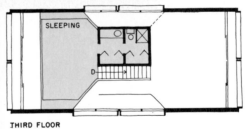

DINING

KIT.

U

D

SITTING

SECOND FLOOR

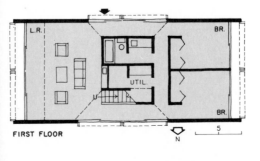

L.R.

BR.

UTIL.

BR.

FIRST FLOOR

SLEEPING

K.

DINING

LIVING

CHILDREN'S BEDROOMS

Alternating platforms above the ground floor (section left) create two-story spaces in the living room (below) and the dining room (above) The interior kitchen, open at both ends (right), is well-ventilated and has a good view of activities in the living room as well as outside on the terrace and the adjacent beach.

Marcel Breuer, Andover, Massachusetts
1956

Utilitarian forms and materials certainly no longer need justification as sensible, economical tools of design. However, placed in the knowing hands of a good architect, neither need they imply coldness or austerity. Simple devices can create fresh types of enrichment—textures, patterns, colors, and above all, constantly changing highlights and shadows—that give a delight parallel to that associated by many with ornament of the past.

The owners of this house in Andover, Massachusetts, were obviously very appreciative of this quality in Marcel Breuer's work when they commissioned him to design a new home. It was their third venture into contemporary architecture; their previous house, which adjoins this one, was also extremely attractive.

Andover is a typical New England town, full of tradition and spirit. Federal and Georgian buildings face white and red brick facades onto tree-studded streets. It is primarily a quiet residential community, and one is quite soon in the hilly countryside.

Land for this house is next to the site of the Grieco's last house, which looked out under a pergola thickly hung with grape clusters. Both lots share a naturally beautiful situation with a sweeping view of the countryside. The house fits neatly into a hillside, which slopes very gently down from the road until the entrance courtyard of the house is reached, then falls away, allowing room for a lower floor.

Requirements as to the amount of space and arrangement of rooms had not changed from their previous house. The Griecos are a retired business man and his wife, who have grown children, and who love gardening. They wanted their bedrooms opening onto a dressing-corridor on one side, a private terrace on the other; and a guest room with its own entrance, which could be completely separated from the rest of the house, so the children or guests could come and go at will.

The new Grieco house has a bi-nuclear plan—living and sleeping wings, separated by an entrance hall and central outdoor living terrace. The sleeping end of the house is designed according to the owners' specifications. Bedrooms open onto a yard sheltered by a low stone wall and planting. The living room is ori-

ented toward the west to face the view. Windows are protected from the sun by an exterior louvered canopy, supported by stainless steel cables attached to four masts along the face of the building.

Guest room, bath and garage are placed on a lower floor beneath the living room, to give the required privacy and take advantage of the sloping site. Instead of a separate delivery entrance, there is a service pass-through from the entrance court into the utility room. Marcel Breuer considers the house and plan to be "a good standard solution for married couples whose children are grown."

Since they were admittedly very happy living in their previous house next door, Breuer's first question after being approached to plan them a new one was, "Why do you want to build another house?" The answer was simply that they admired "Breuer Architecture" so much that they wanted to experience living in it!

GRIECO RESIDENCE, Andover, Massachusetts. Architect: *Marcel Breuer*. Contractor: *George Fichera*.

Combinations of materials, so often misused, can add sparkle and interest to a crisp design when handled with the subtle restraint of this example: fieldstone is played against board and batten, glass and the strong sunshade pattern.

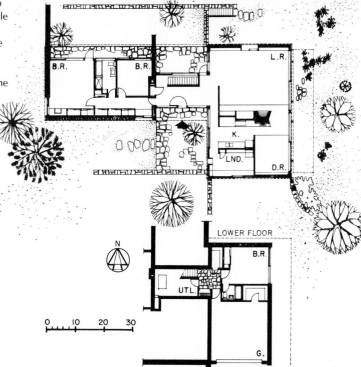

L.R.

B.R.   B.R.

K.

LND.   D.R.

LOWER FLOOR

N

B.R.

UTL.

G.

0   10   20   30

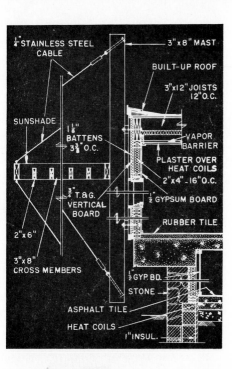

¼" STAINLESS STEEL CABLE

3"x8" MAST

BUILT-UP ROOF

3"x12" JOISTS 12"O.C.

SUNSHADE

1⅛" BATTENS 3½"O.C.

VAPOR BARRIER

PLASTER OVER HEAT COILS

2"x4"-16"O.C.

½ GYPSUM BOARD

¾" T.&G. VERTICAL BOARD

RUBBER TILE

2"x6"

3"x8" CROSS MEMBERS

½ GYP. BD.

STONE

ASPHALT TILE

HEAT COILS

1" INSUL.

The thrust of the house from its rocky perch is especially evident in the two views from the valley, above: The photograph at left shows the study end of the gallery while the one above it shows the entrance. The cantilevered living room, far right, has a deck and is entered from the gallery, right, as are most other rooms.

Eliot Noyes
Fairfield County, Connecticut
1971

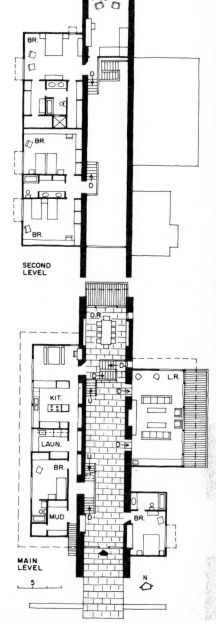

SECOND LEVEL

MAIN LEVEL

Set on a rocky mound overlooking a wooded valley near Stamford, Connecticut, this spacious house is a splendid platform from which to observe the daily progress of the seasons.

In order to minimize the difficulty of building upon the ledge rock, Eliot Noyes chose to build two massive, parallel stone-concrete walls from which the various rooms cantilever on post-tensioned concrete beams. The 14-foot wide central gallery, in which owner Robert Graham can display objets d'art from his New York City gallery is seen by Noyes as an indoor street. One moves through the stone walls into rooms as if he were entering separate houses from a narrow alley. It is a scheme with which Noyes has experimented for a long time.

Thus the plan can be seen as a variation upon Noyes' own famous house: two separate houses across a garden wrapped by a stone wall. Here the garden (ivy has been

planted in the crevices of the walls) is enclosed by the stone walls and the two houses are outside the enclosure. The gallery also serves as a lively ballroom when an orchestra plays from the study during parties.

The three-foot thick walls were built using three-foot high slipforms which ran the entire length of the walls, 94 feet long. Heavy steel mesh, 8 inches in from each side of the form was wired to vertical steel rods. Selected rocks were pushed into place between the mesh and the form. Concrete was then poured from the center and allowed to seep out to the form through the stones. When the concrete had hardened, the forms were raised and the operation repeated.

GRAHAM RESIDENCE, Fairfield County, Connecticut. Architect: *Eliot Noyes.* Structural engineer: *Viggo Bonnesen.* Mechanical engineer: *John L. Alteri.* Landscape architect: *Peter G. Rolland.* Contractor: *Sam Grasso Co.*

Joseph W. Molitor photos

Photos: Green © (ESTO)

Edward Larrabee Barnes

New York State 1968

"Now you see it, now you don't" is a reaction you might have while passing this house in the woods. Which is a response the architect wanted to achieve by nestling the house inconspicuously among the trees. For those who do approach, this crescendo of shed-roofs appears like a forest hamlet.

Representing another step in the evolution of his "woodland houses", here Barnes created a totally unified design—including interiors, which contain furniture (couch, beds and dressers) of his own "elimination of legs" design.

Barnes has designed a varied, but basically horizontal, rambling house. In this case many of the elements are individualized under their own terne-metal shed-roofs.

On a sunny, summer day, with the window-walls open on both sides of the living room and dining-kitchen, the house becomes a large, informal pavilion. Informality is a keynote throughout the house, but it is especially evident in the kitchen, which is well suited for full-family participation in meal preparation.

The living room, with windows open, becomes an interior extension of the balcony. All windows slide open to allow the free movement of air and people, except the triangular ones for which have special casements and sail-like shades.

A long entrance hall connects a self-contained apartment (near photo, top) with the rest of the house (center photo, top). A walk down this hall gives an indication of what surprises to expect further on—lively variances in ceiling heights and light qualities.

Living and play areas are on the main floor, with four bedrooms upstairs off another hall that has stairs at each end.

PRIVATE RESIDENCE, New York State. Architect: *Edward Larrabee Barnes—associate architect: George Large.* Engineers: *William Kaplan: Tom Polise (mechanical): Severud Associates (structural).* Landscape architect: *Peter Rolland.* Contractor: *Louis E. Lee Co.*

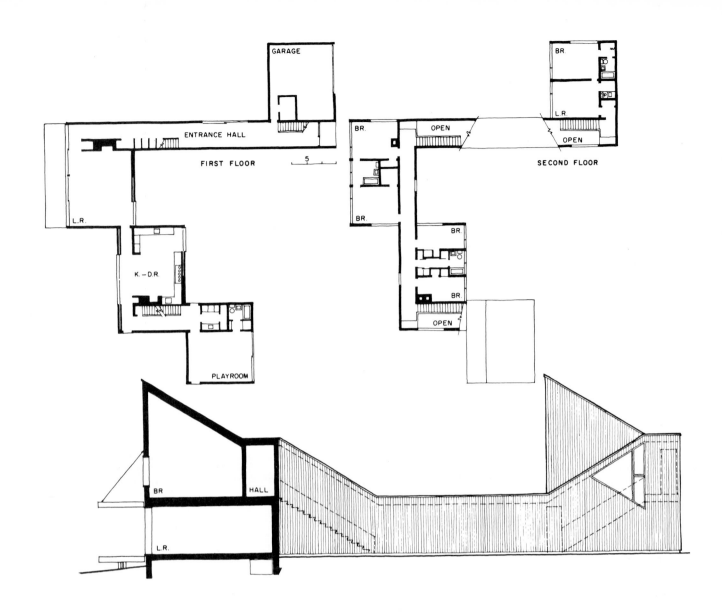

GARAGE

ENTRANCE HALL

FIRST FLOOR   5

L.R.

K.-D.R.

PLAYROOM

BR.

OPEN

BR.

BR.

BR.

BR.

OPEN

SECOND FLOOR

BR.

L.R.

OPEN

BR   HALL

L.R.

Crisp, warm materials, used throughout the house, show in the entrance
hall (photo lower left). In the playroom, a ladder, next to the window
in the photo, lets the children climb
to an attic-like compartment and
hide. Except in the playroom, Barnes
has used quarry-tile throughout the
main floor. Upstairs, all floors are
walnut-stained oak. Downstairs,
when the window-walls are open,
balcony joins living room area.

UPPER FLOOR

MAIN FLOOR

The tall living room gives the house a spaciousness that is surprising given its size. Built-in furniture, interconnected spaces, and large windows looking into the woods in three directions also help expand the space. The section reveals a tiny, secluded roof deck reached by a ladder.

Henri Gueron 1972
East Hampton, New York

Ben Schnall photos

In 1971, architect Henri Gueron built himself this three-bedroom house (including equipment, insulated, and finished interiors, as well as site work) for $15,000.

Gueron lists four ways by which he accomplished this feat: 1. Square footage was kept as low as possible, barely more than the zoning minimum of 975 square feet; 2. The house was designed on a 4- by 8-foot module, horizontally and vertically, since standard-size plywood was the ideal material for his design—both economically and esthetically; 3. Almost all prefabricated elements are also standard (the principal exception is the acrylic dome in the dining area which cost $110); 4. He served as his own general contractor for an estimated saving of 20 per cent and detailed the house to be easy to build. He estimates that done for a client using standard contract procedures, the cost would have been about $25,000.

The crisp exterior is ⅜-in. resin-impregnated plywood applied to the studs. The caulking is a white elasto-meric sealant. Two coats of latex acrylic semi-gloss paint were used both on the exterior and on the dry-wall interiors. Finally, the bright accent colors of epoxy enamel were added. Placed diagonally on a long narrow lot studded with the scrub oak typical of eastern Long Island, the house is invisible from the road in summer but during the gray winter provides a brilliant flash of color for passers-by.

Architect and *owner:* Henri Gueron of Gueron and Lepp. *Location:* East Hampton, New York. *Engineer:* Ken Smith (electrical).

SECTION A-A

William Morgan
Northern Florida
1977

Architect William Morgan has long been an exponent of buildings that blend with the landscape by bringing the surrounding terrain up around and even over them. This is not to say that the resulting forms do not have a definite presence; he will quickly draw comparisons to the ancient monumental architecture of local Indian tribes, which he points out was not that much different in sophistication than say that of the Incas—or even Egyptians in the Middle Dynasties. One of the real fascinations in Morgan's buildings (including houses) is that they are at once monumental beyond most peers and exceptionally respectful of their natural surroundings.

Located on an Atlantic beach of northern Florida, this latest "earthform" house has been designed for a couple with three children, and—in recognition of its site—bears marked differences from Morgan's earlier houses, which tend to be enclosed by their bermed surroundings. The more open qualities demanded by the location are achieved by an opening of the side toward the ocean. Here, the local norm of an often prosaic and "tacked-on" screen-covering for the swimming pool becomes part of the basic form. It reveals the panorama of the beach in a startling and dramatic contrast to the enclosed interior and exterior spaces, experienced on entry.

Besides a bedroom and a convertible study-guest room on the first floor, there are three bedrooms on an upper level, which share the living areas' views—berms on the side and front of the house form protective enclosures for the entrance court—partially concealing the cars within, and for courts off of the lower-level bedroom and study—one of which is partially roofed by a solar heater. This house contains 2,800 square feet of enclosed space.

PRIVATE RESIDENCE, Florida. Architect: *William Morgan*. Structural engineers: *Haley W. Keister Associates, Inc.* Mechanical engineer: *Roy Turknett Engineers.* Contractor: *Dave Plummer Construction Co.*

Photos: Alexandre Georges

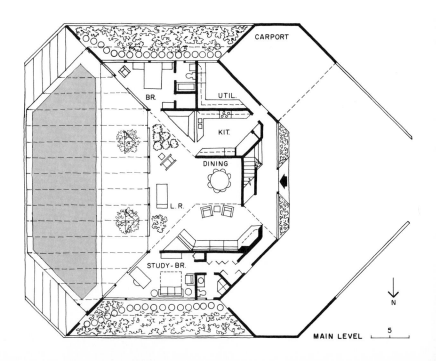

MAIN LEVEL

This "earthform" house carries architect William Morgan's concepts developed inland to the beach. It provides both a sense of openness to ocean views and protection.

Both the retaining walls for the berms and the screen enclosure visually extend the enclosed area of 2800 square feet.

C. Blakeway Millar
Vaughan, Ontario
1980

As inventive in its planning as it is fresh in its images, this extraordinary, four-bedroom house outside Toronto is designed for a client whose family has roots deep in the Canadian lumber business and who asked for a house that made conspicuous use of a variety of wood species. The rough sawn heavy timber frame of the house is jack pine, and it takes shape over a base of masonry that follows the site's falling contours down to a stream and an off-stream pond. The frame is infilled with glass throughout and even the sloping roof sections are 25 per cent skylighted. This degree of openness would be implausible in a climate with harsh winters had the architect not developed simple but effective environmental controls. The skylights, for instance, are equipped with insulated louvers that are operated with a pulley and cord system, and can be closed to control heat loss at night or adjusted to serve as baffles against the sun by day. The glazed infill areas on all elevations get a winter covering of 3-inch-thick insulated panels mounted on pivots so that they open like oriental screens. In most areas, the panels are finished in plywood. In the living room, they are covered in suede and hung with pictures. All panels are vented to the inside to relieve the effects of condensation and trapped air expansion. These

panels, together with the skylight louvers, can achieve insulating values to R-25.

The house is heated by a combination of furnace, fireplace, and woodburning stoves. Warm air is collected at the top of the house, recirculated by fans through the ridge collector duct to electric furnaces, then returned to the living spaces. In summer, a cooling cycle is activated and warm air is drawn off at the top of the house and vented at the northwest corner.

The structural boxes at the gable ends enclose the ends of the sloping roof's gutter system. As the frame has little or no diagonal bracing, these box forms also serve as structural stiffeners.

PRIVATE RESIDENCE, Vaughan, Ontario. Architects: *C. Blakeway Millar*—project architects: *D. Alvisi, B. McCulloch.* Structural engineers: *Morrison, Herschfield, Burgess, Huggins.* Foundations: *Golder Associates.* Mechanical engineers: *Engineering Interface.* Interiors: *Sandra J. Millar.* Cost Consultant: Anthony Wallis Associates. Contractor: *G. Faion and Sons.*

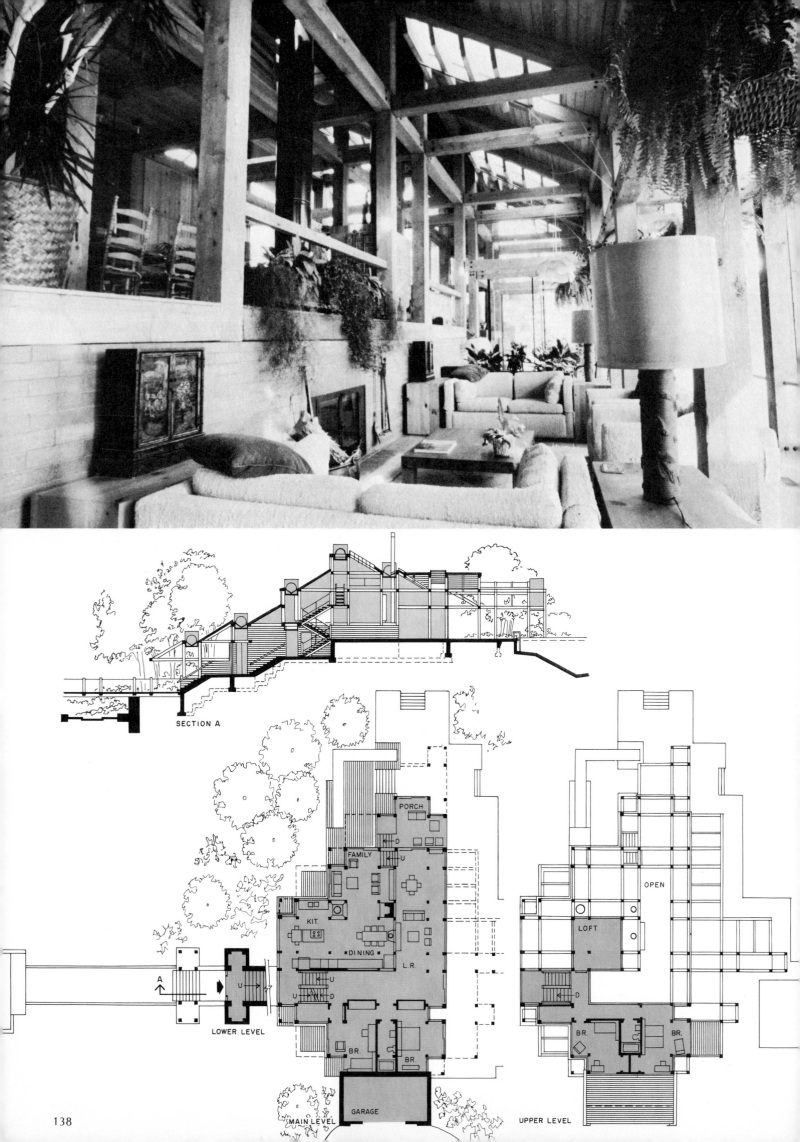

SECTION A

LOWER LEVEL

PORCH

FAMILY

KIT.

DINING

L.R.

BR.

BR.

GARAGE

MAIN LEVEL

OPEN

LOFT

BR.

BR.

UPPER LEVEL

The heavy timber frame provides the rhythmic pattern that separates the house into its component spaces. Where required for privacy, infill panels of plywood or plank are set into position within the frame. Textures vary between the rough-sawn heavy timbers and the fine-grained white pine of the kitchen floor and cabinets. Quarry tile is used on the floor of the living room. The house is furnished and detailed in rough and rustic character. In time, the exteriors will weather naturally to the silvery tones of neighboring farm buildings.

5. THERE'S NOTHING NEW ABOUT

Sometimes, in the midst of the current verbosity about "modern is dead" and the "post-modernist" infatuation with historic allusion, one feels that an entire generation neither studied architectural history nor the modern period since World War II except for a very limited selection of the highlights.

The cold truth is that historicism and electicism in houses never really died in the U.S.—or anywhere else for that matter. And modern (or "contemporary" as most have called the style since the late 40s) is vigorous and far from dead now.

In spite of the fervor of contemporary architects in searching for simplified, original and innovative design, in absolute numbers the larger portion of houses built through the 1950s, and even later, were highly eclectic, whether custom–designed or builder-development houses. Many of them did, however, gradually incorporate many (if not most) of the innovative new ideas. A drive through practically any U.S. suburb or a glance through the shelter and builder magazines of the period will amply bear this out. In the midst of a growing interest in modernism, there were some potent counter forces—among them Hollywood films (especially "Gone with the Wind"), the Williamsburg and the other much-publicized restorations of the 1930s, the employment of many U.S. architects for the Historic Buildings Survey during the Great Depression, and the popularity of the "Cape Cod" houses by architect Royal Barry Wills and later, the houses of Levittown.

On the other hand, the International Style of modernism—highly codified and replete with manifestos in Europe by the late 1920s, so labeled by Henry Russell Hitchcock and Philip Johnson in their book of that name in 1932, and further reinforced in the subsequent Museum of Modern Art exhibit in New York—had gone through a significant metamorphosis by the end of World War II. The apogee of the International Style—a taut-skinned, white plastered, ribbon-windowed, asymmetrically facaded cube—was tempered with "allusions" (to use the current buzz-word) to exotic, foreign and historic

recall, and to a significant amount of regionalism.

There were certainly many reasons for this—through the ages, no architectural style has remained static for long—but two are particularly obvious. One is the architectural education in the U.S. schools of that period. Most architectural faculties made the transition from Beaux Arts historicism to Bauhaus modernity slowly, sometimes piece-meal, so that often both methods and points of view were taught concurrently, with students working in and absorbing each. Even the Beaux Arts Institute in New York—with which many schools retained a connection—did not change its name to the National Institute for Architectural Education until some years later. The enthusi-

HISTORY

"Landmarks Commission, I think!"

asms for innovation obviously waxed—but there was a tempering foundation of more classical ways and a thorough grounding in Western architectural history. (However, Near-Eastern, Asian and American Indian buildings were usually too quickly covered in curriculums and texts as "Non-Historic Styles".)

A second big factor was the travelling architect's direct exposure to buildings all over the world—researching both the monuments and the indigenous houses everywhere. World War II, which was truly global, played a huge part in this for architects (and budding ones) who were in the services—and the subsequent development of air travel made possible continued researches. And, of course, as with any travel, one looks at home with a sharper eye on return, and local regional qualities are more readily appreciated.

The direct effects of these influences most quickly surfaced in house design—if only because houses can be more quickly planned and constructed than more sizeable buildings. In the introductory article for *Record Houses* of 1958, these trends had become strong enough for us to show photos of some of the houses along with those of some clearly related influences: Japanese roofs, Chinese compounds, Roman atriums, Spanish grilles, Indian fretwork, the English Stately Home,

neo-classic symmetry, Mykonos-like truncated cubes. And—closer to home—New England covered bridges, Southern colonnades, neo-Georgian recalls, Northeastern shingles. The list is endless, and a lot of the houses shown throughout this book reflect them—not just those chosen for this chapter.

Nor has the interest and activity in restoration, renovation, "retrofit"—or whatever you want to call it—ever been far away since the days of the Williamsburg restoration. The movement to save and preserve individual historic houses has been constant, and expanded into our current concern with conserving houses of more modest virtue and charm for their simple nostalgic appeal.

Perhaps, as some contend, the new houses actually built in the early 1970s were a bit more restrained in direct recall or allusion than the preceding decades—though one could possibly make a case that the Corbusian ones of some 50 years before, which inspired new work by Charles Gwathmey, Richard Meier and others, are just that. But does the reality lie in the fact that, as eclectic houses became more modern and modern houses more eclectic, there is a real rapprochement of design rationale to (and *into*) history? That modern is not dead, but has finally synthesized into general public taste?

Keck & Keck
Chicago, Illinois
1967

Photos: Hedrich-Blessing

This multi-level town-house, with many of the advantages of a house in the country, is a fine example of the renewal of interest in individual city houses by families who want to live near the center of town and its cultural activities, and who don't want to drive or commute long miles each day into the country for a view of trees and grass. The Karlin house, a sizeable one for a family of five, was planned with this in mind, on a 50-foot lot in the middle of Chicago's Hyde Park (near the University of Chicago). Ample play and garden space is provided—even terraces for each of the top-floor bedrooms. On the general trend, the Kecks, who designed the house, comment that families "should have this right of choice, but in general, planning commissions allocate little land for individual houses in or near the center of cities, an unfortunate oversight in planning. Urban renewal is helping somewhat in such planning—however, it could do better than it has in the past."

The Kecks, however, have done very well, indeed, in providing a great feeling of space and privacy in this house, which is set among three-story walk-ups and high-rise buildings. The exterior design, sophisticated as it is in black brick, white trim and copper roof, is handled in restrained contemporary manner to blend with the neighborhood.

On the interior, the sense of space is tremendously increased by using a multi-level scheme, with many of the spaces opening into each other as balconies or split levels. The house is completely air conditioned both summer and winter, with an electronic-type air cleaner to minimize dirt and dust. Thus, most of the "problems" of city living are well provided for.

KARLIN HOUSE, Chicago, Illinois. Owners: *Mr. and Mrs. Norman Karlin.* Architects: *George Fred Keck—William Keck Architects.* Contractor: *Nathan Linn & Sons.*

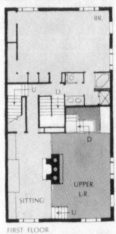

SECOND FLOOR

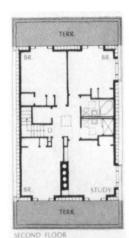

FIRST FLOOR

GROUND FLOOR

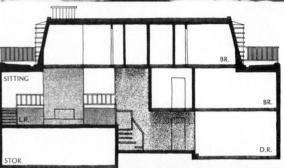

Hugh Newell Jacobsen
Washington, D.C.
1969

Located amid the historic architecture of a quiet, tree-lined Georgetown street, this Washington, D.C. townhouse shows well that residential design can be contemporary and innovative, while respectful of an established neighborhood.

The architect's solution uses timeless materials in their natural state—burgundy-colored brick and gray slate—to keep the texture, scale and rhythm of the existing street. Materials combine with new interpretation of the traditional arch, bay window and mansard roof for a forceful design statement, in which the sculptured front bay windows especially are thoroughly modern in their expression of interior space.

Rooms were designed by the architect for a dramatic and uncluttered look usually found in a much larger house. Living room furnishings include silk and molded plastic or leather and chrome chairs. Floors are stained oak. Front rooms—the dining room and kitchen on the second floor and the master bedroom on the third—have a view of a park across the street. Back rooms—second-floor living room and other bedrooms—face a private garden. All are also oriented to two circular stair towers, which form the visual focal points of the house. Each stairwell includes view-through openings, and is capped with a 10-foot plastic dome to bring sunlight down through all the house. White walls and designed lighting add to the expansive quality of the scheme, which packs a great deal of comfort into an urban lot, thus offering its owners many qualities of a detached, suburban house with the many advantages of urban living.

The traditional townhouse, which fulfills a contemporary need, has, in this very spirited design, found a thoroughly contemporary expression.

Behind their brick house, the owners can enjoy a secluded garden, equipped with fountain and slate floors on two levels and giving onto the living room via sliding aluminum doors. Kitchen and dining room are two steps up, a story above the entry. Special curved bricks were architect-designed.

Robert C. Lautman photos

RESIDENCE FOR MR. AND MRS. STEVEN TRENTMAN, Washington, D.C. Architect: *Hugh Newell Jacobsen.* Engineer: *James Madison Cutts.* Landscape architect: *Lester Collins.* Interiors: *Hugh Jacobsen.* Contractor: *The Brincefield Company.*

This townhouse by architect Hugh Jacobsen is only 24 feet wide, but includes built-ins and floor-to-ceiling glass for an uncluttered, spacious look. Operable panels on the sides of stepped-out windows are for ventilation. Bookshelves act as elements to expand space.

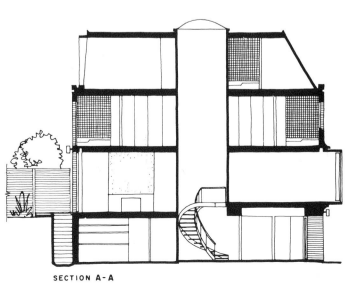

SECTION A-A

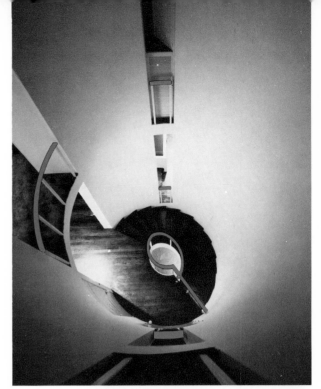

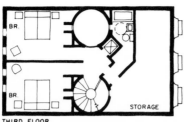

BR.

BR.

STORAGE

THIRD FLOOR

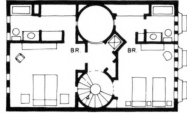

BR.

BR.

SECOND FLOOR

A

K.

A

L.R.

D.R.

MAIN FLOOR

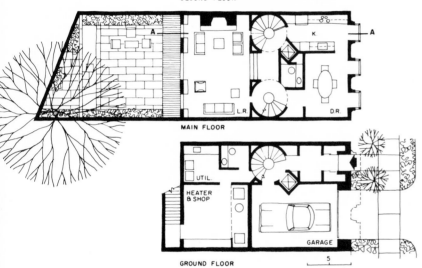

UTIL.

HEATER & SHOP

GARAGE

GROUND FLOOR

5

Strategically placed lighting fixtures—wall washers for living room, recessed units for kitchen—are integral to the design. Circular stairwell begins at entry and becomes a light shaft at the first floor, with spiral stairs resuming in opposite well.

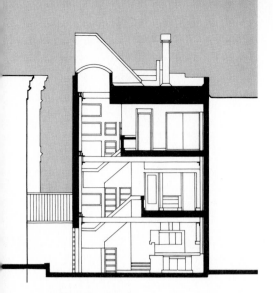

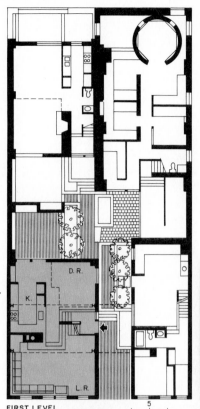

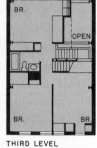

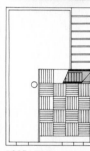

FIRST LEVEL   5   SECOND LEVEL   THIRD LEVEL   ROOF LEVEL

BRHB
Philadelphia
Pennsylvania
1979

From a rather ordinary, turn-of-the century urban building, last used as a candy factory (photo upper right), the architects have carved an office for themselves and four condominium apartments. The house shown here—the most elaborate of the four—is for architect-owner F. Cecil Baker. Baker's house extends upward through three floors with entry, kitchen, living and dining space on the lowest floor. The intermediate floor includes master bedroom and study overlooking the dining space (photo lower right), while the upper level is given over to additional bedrooms. The spectacular well space, filled with daylight from skylights in the roof, gives the design a drama and verticality seldom achieved in residential design.

The building's original steel structure was retained and used to express the essential volumetric organization. New walls were added where needed, and those requiring insulation were treated with a sand-finished plaster over sprayed-on insulation.

The owners of the four houses and the office make a condominium community. They share certain amenities and costs. Not the least of the advantages of the reciprocal arrangement is that the presence of office occupants gives the houses an important measure of security by day and vice versa at night.

The detailing is exceptionally thoughtful throughout and deserves the reader's attention.

CANDY FACTORY COURT, Philadelphia, Pennsylvania. Architects: *Baker Rothschild Horn Blyth—partner-in-charge: F. Cecil Baker.* Contractor: *BRHB Developers.*

Photos: Tom Crane

The living room (photos above) overlooks the street. The original steel girders and wood joists were retained, as was the brickwork. The Mexican floor tile is new. In the master bedroom (photo right) the bath tub is screened by a glass block partition. Child's room (photo left) is on the third level. A great deal of study and attention went into detailing these spaces as the photos amply demonstrate.

Paul Rudolph

Athens, Alabama

1965

The architecture of the South, most vividly characterized by the neoclassical period, has been dramatically restated and revitalized by Paul Rudolph in this imposing southern villa. Despite the dominant use of classical forms, the repetition of the curved shape in stairways and balconies evokes a certain romantic aura. The stairs seem made for the sweep of a ball gown, and the balconies for twilight serenades.

The house is set on a podium from which rise the 32 circular brick columns. A long, curved drive leads to the front of the house, which is for the most part solid and quite private. Curved steps on the south side take one to the entry. The almost startling whiteness of the house set against the surrounding greenery is once again typical of neoclassical southern homes.

WALLACE RESIDENCE, Athens, Alabama. Owners: *Mr. and Mrs. John Wallace*. Architect: *Paul Rudolph*. Structural engineer: *John Altieri*. Mechanical engineer: *Herman J. Spiegel*.

Photos: Alexandre Georges

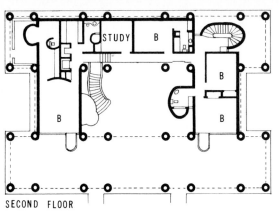

SECOND FLOOR

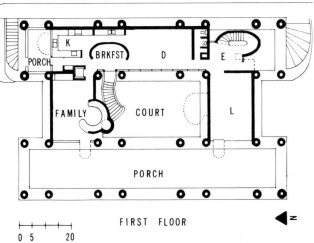

FIRST FLOOR

0 5 20

N

The central court, around which the whole of the Wallace house is planned, is perhaps the most imposing part of the design. Here all the different elements in the design are brought together; curved stairs, columns, the long porch can all be clearly seen from the court. As this area is open to the sky, variations of bright sunlight and deep shadow are seen here to full advantage.

Describing the structure of the house, the architect said, "The materials are unified, cement-like; brick exterior and plaster interior, although marble from an old Alabama courthouse was installed where cost would allow. The columns are not made of special radial brick but standard brick laid on edge." The house has a wood stud frame and floor joists and a builtup roof. Off-white plaster interior surfaces enhance some very nice period furniture. The cost was $90,000.

Winston Elting
Ligonier, Pennsylvania

1965

Although "Stornoway" is a country house very much in the contemporary idiom, it nevertheless has strong roots in a tradition of country house design dating as far back as feudal times. The imagination of many of today's leading architects has been caught by village and farm house designs in Europe, and a number of them have translated these forms into modern techniques and materials and have used them as a basis for their personal architectural expression. Concern with shed roofs, concentration on light and shade, high sloping ceilings, often with skylights in the roof angles, are typical of this approach and can be seen in Winston Elting's strongly individualistic handling of an accepted theme.

Approaching the house through rolling farm country and entering the paved courtyard as the afternoon sun throws long shadows on the granite paving and the stone walls are mellow in the sunlight, one has the impression of com-

ing to a house which has been an integral part of its surroundings for many years. It is almost the feeling that one might have on approaching a farm house in the Cotswolds. The unself-conscious regional quality of the house was quite deliberate and was in fact built into the program, which stated that the house, though very large, should appear to belong to the natural landscape and should at all costs avoid the overpowering impression of a large estate. The use of local stone for the walls, the quiet dark gray terne roof, the massing of the building around a central courtyard, are all factors in the architect's success in meeting his client' requirements.

"STORNOWAY," Ligonier, Pennsylvania. Architect: *Winston Elting—associate architect: Robert H. Burdett.* Engineers: *G. A. Mattern & Associates.* Landscape architects: *Franz Lipp & Associates.* Interior decorator: *Catherine G. Rawson.* Contractor: *F. Hoffman Co.*

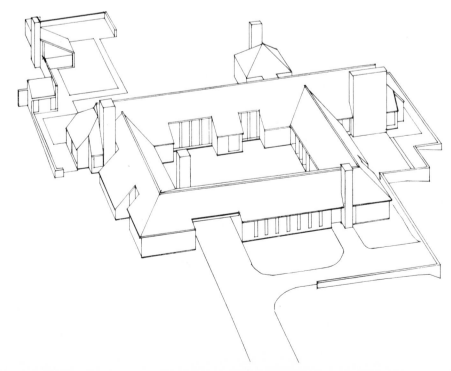

To accommodate second story windows without the need for dormers and to maintain the uniformity of the roof pitch, the stone walls have been recessed at these points. This has the effect of putting the exterior walls on two or more planes and creates an unusual play of light and shadow. Inside the house, the narrow windows with the stone detailing between them, rough stone walls and fireplaces, which contrast effectively with the light-colored sand-float plaster of the other interior wall surfaces, create an impression of warmth and intimacy without in any way detracting from the wonderful sense of space.

Although the house has a pleasant, informal, rambling quality, the plan is sufficiently compact to work very well as a complete unit. The variety of forms have a logic and cohesion which enable them to operate visually and functionally as an integrated whole.

Photos: Joseph W. Molitor

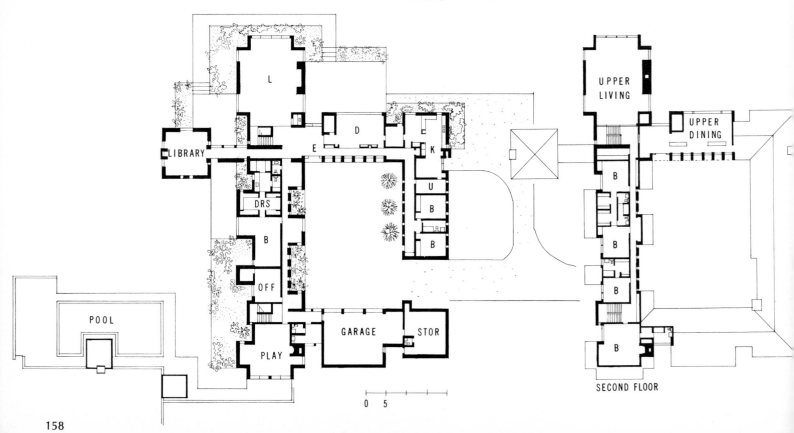

SECOND FLOOR

0   5

Milton Weinstock photos

Wooden panels roll across the large glazed areas on the first floor (photos at top on facing page) when the owners are away; and stack neatly, below.

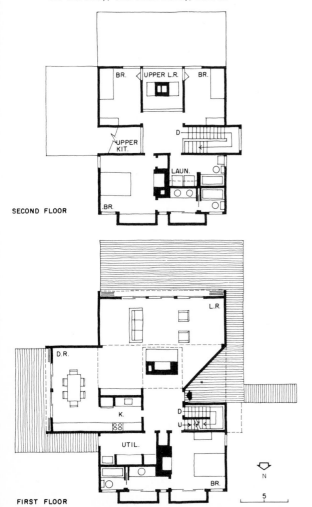

SECOND FLOOR

FIRST FLOOR

Mills & Martin
Dublin, New Hampshire
1971

The austere, four-square self-sufficiency of the traditional American farmhouse is evoked by the exterior of this vacation house in Dublin, New Hampshire. Yet the interior, organized around the same central hall as the farmhouse, is rich in openness, informality and spatial variety.

In many ways, the problems facing those who build in northern New Hampshire have not changed in two hundred years. Therefore, the resemblance to old wood buildings is not surprising. Narrow cedar clapboards, parallel to the roof, and generous cornerboards, clearly traditional, are here used to emphasize the sweep of the two low wings away from the solid two-story main block. The diagonals at once tie the building to the land and thrust the matching half-gables to the sky.

This articulation of the gable, not to be found in old farm houses to be sure, permits a clerestory above the second floor hall. This unexpected, almost invisible light source fills the top of the house, the stairway, the kitchen and the two-story space around the chimney with light on the dreariest day.

The living room, right, conveys the clarity of the internal organization. A substantial wood and steel truss, spanning 26 feet, supports the structure and allows the chimney of the ironspot brick fireplace to stand free in the eight-foot square space. Thus in even such an intensely planned house, one can share from the upper hall or the children's bedrooms, the activities on the lower floor.

Architects: Willis N. Mills, Jr. and Timothy Martin. *Owners:* Mr. and Mrs. Daniel Burnham. *Location:* Dublin, New Hampshire. *Structural engineer:* Paul Pantano. *Mechanical engineer:* Sanford O. Hess. *Contractor:* Bergeron Construction Co.

E. Fay Jones
Arkansas
1978

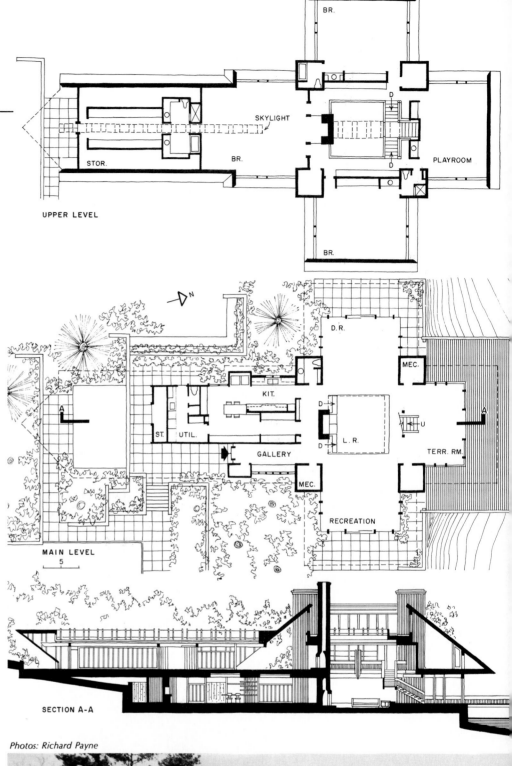

UPPER LEVEL

D.R.

MEC.

KIT.

ST. UTIL.

GALLERY

MEC.

L. R.

TERR. RM.

RECREATION

MAIN LEVEL

SECTION A-A

Photos: Richard Payne

Long low lines with deeply sloping roofs, cantilevered overhangs and an expansive open plan, all combined with a sensitive respect for landscape and reverence for the nature of materials, powerfully recall Frank Lloyd Wright's Prairie Style; and indeed architect Fay Jones, who designed this house in central Arkansas, did study for a time at Taliesin. Closer observation, however, tempers the initial impression and suggests rather that a proper application of Wrightian principles allows an architect to remain very much his own man and to design buildings of individuality. (Mr. Jones, queried about the Wrightian aspects of his design, demurred politely while granting certain "intangible" influences. "As a matter of fact," he said, "those service cores remind me a little of Louis Kahn's servant spaces.")

The house, built for a couple with two young sons, is partially sunk into the shore of a private man-made lake and extended over the water on concrete pilings. Its cruciform plan places a two-story living room at the crossing, from which radiate living spaces downstairs and children's rooms upstairs. The strongest defining elements of the plan are four large structural service cores, sheathed with plywood and battens, which support the truss-like cantilevers of the radiating bedrooms and a second-floor gallery that encircles the living room.

Though the steep sheltering roofs suggest from the exterior a perhaps darkened house, the interior is in fact extraordinarily open to light and views of the water and landscape. Entertainment areas on the first floor beneath the cantilevers are glazed on three sides, affording the living room a 180-degree view interrupted only by the square columns. Upstairs, triangular glass end walls open each bedroom on two sides. Extensive skylights above the central well and master suite admit additional daylight, as do clerestories connecting the four towers. To reinforce this openness, glass is mitered at the corners of the downstairs rooms and at the ridge of the skylights.

The entry and the second-floor gallery provide exhibition space for the owners' collection of Indian art and relics.

PRIVATE RESIDENCE, Arkansas. Architects: *Fay E. Jones*—project assistants: *John Womack and Maurice Jennings.* Mechanical engineer: *James Wellons.* Landscape architects: *Landscape Associates, Inc.* Contractor: *Herb Davis.*

Smith & Williams, Pasadena, California
1956

In most good neighborhoods, there is at least one solitary plot lying fallow and dispirited because, due to some topographical quirk, it has been considered too difficult or expensive to build on. Grading, filling or complex foundations *can* cost a lot, and as a result, relatively flat open land is generally sought-after for economical houses. But, in spite of the cliffs, ravines, or what have you, that mark these neglected tracts, they may have more scenic beauty—and are usually considerably lower in cost than adjoining sites.

Without resorting to any extreme eccentricities of structure or design, the architects of this house for Mr. and Mrs. Robert Crowell, in Pasadena, California, have devised a very good one-story answer for such a problem site. The house

also harbors a number of planning ideas for any type of plot. Worth particular note is its Japanese aura; whether consciously striven for or not, it is becoming a significant trend, perhaps because of its blending of modesty with great style.

The peculiarities of the lot include a very steep slope, and a large amount of filled ground on the flat area near the street. The slope is heavily wooded, offering a nearly idyllic privacy, and it overlooks a meandering creek at its base. Tracts in the area carry restrictions requiring a minimum house size of 3500 square feet, or four family bedrooms, and resistance to earthquakes. Pasadena, of course, is balmy, tree-studded, rolling, and its people delight in informal outdoor living.

To adjust to the site condition, the house proper was constructed on flat filled ground near the street. Caissons were employed for grade beams, using existing grade and forms (no expensive special wood forms were needed). Extra living space was gained outdoors by building a deck of lighter, less expensive construction out over the slope.

The structure is economical, has great clarity; a modular system of posts and beams at four-foot intervals is used throughout. All walls not required to resist horizontal sheer for earthquake loads were eliminated. The remaining spaces between posts are filled with glass panes or louvers. Panels are clear, translucent or opaque—depending on outlook and exposure. The plan is well organized, circulation good;

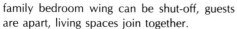

Photos: Julius Shulman

family bedroom wing can be shut-off, guests are apart, living spaces join together.

Smith and Williams felt that the "problem of an uneven site in relationship to the level of the floor would be best expressed architecturally by a clear delineation of the floor line. We cantilevered house walls one foot beyond the grade beam and ran a continuous sill around the building. The result: shadow and sharp emphasis of the line."

The Crowells and their teen-age son required a one floor house with a large living room, four bedrooms (one would serve for guests, study or a maid), and a family TV room with flexible partition opening on living or dining room. They dislike fussy ornament. Say the Crowells: "The house takes full advantage of the best outlook

SHINGLES
1"x6" STRIPPING
1" INSULATION
2"x6" T&G

4"x4" RAFTER

⅝" DOWEL

4"x4" POST

2"x6" T&G

4"x6" GIRDER
4'-0 O.C.

B.R.

B.R.

N

B.R.

BAR
FAM.
PTR
B.R.
L.R.
D.R.
BKFST
K.
UTL.

0   10   20   30

The back of the Crowell house seems vast, open, with deck extending living area into tree tops. Exterior rolling slat blinds and overhangs shield glass walls from sun; stained glass panes give interesting accents. Section shows simplicity of structure. Landscaping deftly echoes the character of the house.

and protects privacy; closeness to the outdoors is quite relaxing. Everything is convenient, comfortable and easy to care for. We like the simplicity and straight lines, the soft look and variation in color and grain of the stained redwood."

CROWELL RESIDENCE, Pasadena, California. Owners: *Mr. and Mrs. Robert Crowell.* Architects: *Smith and Williams.* Landscape architects: *Eckbo, Roylston & Williams.* Contractor: *William C. Crowell Co.*

Hugh
Newell
Jacobsen
Chevy Chase
Maryland
1977

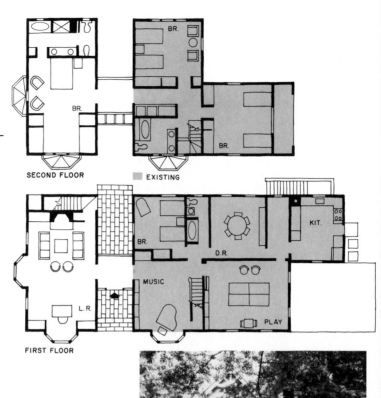

SECOND FLOOR　　■ EXISTING

FIRST FLOOR

Few readers will recognize Hugh Jacobsen's touch in the exterior of this remodeled Victorian house in a suburb of Washington, D.C. The original portion of this house was built in 1871 as an outbuilding to a larger house of similar style. The main house was long ago erased by a change in the street plan, but the small house remained, surviving several owners and a series of modest alterations.

When the present owner purchased the property in 1975, Hugh Jacobsen was retained to make a new addition and to thoroughly modernize the interiors. But because the neighborhood was old, the corner site prominent, and the Victorian character of the design so lovingly preserved through earlier alterations, Jacobsen carried out the new exterior work using the old mold—or carefully studied reproductions of that mold. The original entry with its covered porch was removed. A floor-to-ceiling bay window was substituted and then repeated on the new wing. Window trim, fenestration and eave details were carefully researched as were paint colors used in small country houses of the 1870s. Both in the old exterior and in the addition, the ethos of the earlier era was preserved, including the promise of well proportioned, carefully developed spaces within.

On the inside, however, the Old Queen would not have found herself at home. The house is fully air conditioned and the interior development of the spaces, their arrangement, their furnishing are pure Jacobsenian. Starting with the glass entry link, and continuing across two floors, the house is contemporary and equipped with all the appurtenances of modern life.

There is always a special feeling about houses in which the old and the new are beautifully harmonized. Here this harmony is achieved very purposefully through a process of historical allusion that, as recently as five years ago, might have been unthinkable for most architects and even today takes courage and sensitivity.

REMODELING AND ADDITION, Chevy Chase, Maryland. Architect: *Hugh Newell Jacobsen.* Structural engineers: *Kraas & Mok.* Contractor: *Owner.*

The small photo (above) shows the original portion of the small house. The entrance, across a porch, leads into what is now the music room (photo lower right). The living room (photo below) and bedroom above make up the new addition.

"Sheer genius! What Pollock did for painting, he's doing for architecture."

6. EVER-CHANGING, CONFLICTING

Highly condensed architectural histories (as well as the current architectural fads and fashions promoted by the press) all too often lead one to the conclusion that design always follows a tidy, single, undulating curve from over-simple to over-elaborate, changing direction when either becomes excessive.

Perhaps a truer picture would be that both simplicity and elaborateness have always existed concurrently—that there are two curves which overlap, one at its zenith as the other is at its nadir as popularity waxes and wanes. And that popularity can be subject to a variety of often non-esthetic reasons—as simple as boredom, and as complex as socio-economics and political or personal philosophies. It would follow that neither the simple nor the elaborate curve is "best" or "worst": if each is done well—each will have its day.

This has certainly been true of contemporary houses in the last few decades, and each of the houses shown in this book had been labeled with the year it received a *Record House* award to indicate the variety of such opposing ideas and concepts that have appeared concurrently each year.

Probably the biggest polarity in contemporary house design might be called the machine versus the craft ethic; crisp, hard-edged design versus a softer, woodsier approach. Both have co-existed together throughout this last quarter-century—and both have often been exceedingly well done.

Other such opposing directions have also been rife: spartan to sybaritic; cozy domesticity to monumental grandeur; future shock to traditional recall; "high-tech" to "shackatecture"; rock-bottom-budget to expense-be-damned.

Though each of these has occasionally appeared more prominently in favor, there has been no decided progression from one to the other.

There has, however, been continued experimentation and invention in these and all kinds of other directions, sometimes with the utmost gravity and quietness, sometimes with a big sense of humor and verve. And there have been all kinds of

philosophies developed and expounded to explain, and sometimes to justify, the various directions and nuances—though one sometimes feels that the design creativity came first, and the philosophy developed after the fact among many of the more talented architects. And, of course, architectural writers and critics have been busily creating labels for each direction.

A number of very good architects have significantly changed or developed their personal stylistic directions since 1956, and in spite of the limited number of the 514 *Record Houses* that could, of necessity, be included in the scope of this book, we have tried to include several significant examples of these changes. Earlier on, Edward Larrabee Barnes was designing his "platform houses"—simple, flat-roofed, white rectangles set on tidily defined, raised terraces; later he had progressed to what he called "woodland" houses—assemblies of multi-shed-roofed units clad in natural wood. John Johansen ranged from his early romantic pink, gold-vaulted house over a stream to a sort of high-tech series of linked units on a wooded cliff. Ulrich Franzen, on the other hand, started relatively high-tech with steel-framed umbrella pavilions and progressed to quite evocative, largely masonry, towered "castles." Charles Moore evolved from designing houses of relatively casual simplicity to having a lot of fun in his own "post-modernist" manner.

Whatever develops in house design in the ensuing years, let us hope they will not run a course of fleeting fashion, but will have—as past *Record Houses* do—a long-lasting, genuine style.

"Merely a matter of jacking it up
—We certainly weren't going to be outdone by the Joneses!"

ESTHETICS

"Architecture dates you—We live in a Happening."

Ulrich Franzen   1967
Long Island
New York

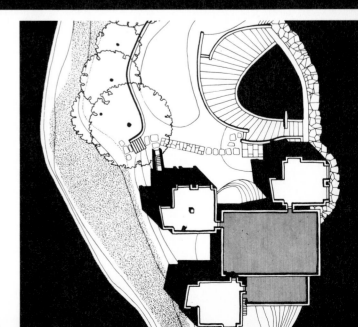

A romantic bastion, strongly constructed by the sea, this house probably marks one of the high points in Ulrich Franzen's individuality of style. In the succession of houses he has designed over the past dozen years, each building has been very innovative, but certain recognizable characteristics have gradually emerged: open pavilions for general living areas, carefully articulated and zoned areas for bedrooms and service, and a great increase in strength of the over-all design. This house is certainly his most ramified to date in each of these directions.

And it makes good sense, given the conditions of the program and site. It is a country or "resort" house for a large family whose major residence is in New York City. Approachable only by a causeway—or by sea—the island site is periodically covered by high tides, and is subject to frequent battering by waves during storms. Franzen has commented that, "the solution therefore raises the living areas a full story above the rocks and permits storm seas to pass underneath the living-dining element; the raised levels of the house permitted siting of the various elements in such a way as to get views not only across Long Island Sound, but up and down a coastline with many inlets."

For all its inherent romanticism, the house has been conceived with a bravura that will probably forestall the architecturally timorous. Once all are used to it, though, the design should wear well and not date rapidly. Outside of the somewhat stylized window and lintel details, it is singularly free of current cliches. And the durable finishes inside and out will certainly fare better than those that depend on a shiny smoothness of surface.

PRIVATE RESIDENCE, Long Island, New York. Architects: *Ulrich Franzen & Associates*. Structural engineer: *William Atlas*. Mechanical engineer: *John Altieri*. Landscape architect: *Charles Middeleer*. Contractor: *E. W. Howell Co.*

Photos: Robert Damora

To withstand the occasional heavy sea action, Franzen constructed the house of heavy reinforced concrete frame. The towers are clad in brick, while exterior walls and parapets of the living and dining room element are exposed architectural concrete. The difference of materials clearly defines the different sections of the building, and helps the constantly changing appearance and massing of the building as one goes around it.

The three towers are almost like separate "houses", each with its own interior staircase. One is for the parents and guests; one has bedrooms for the children; and the third tower contains all the service facilities and a maid's bedroom.

The landscaping for the island has been conceived with much of the same verve as the house and relies largely on the dramatic swimming pool, rock outcroppings, strong retaining walls and groups of sturdy trees.

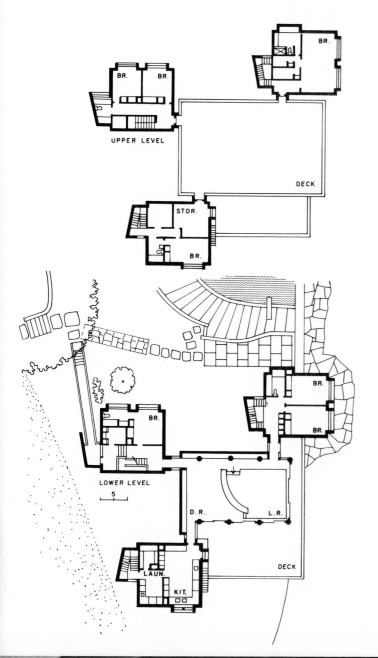

UPPER LEVEL

DECK

STOR.

BR.

LOWER LEVEL

5

DECK

D.R.

L.R.

LAUN.

KIT.

BR.

Photos: George Cserna

Wendell H. Lovett
Bellevue Washington 1969

The strong shapes of this compact house closely echoes the site, and affords beautiful views of Lake Sammamish and the Cascade Mountains. As the setting is fairly open, the design of the house organizes solid walls and windows to give privacy from the road, openness to the view. The crisp, angular silhouette of the house is emphasized against the sky by the use of dark brown cedar siding, and copper for flashing and entrance roof.

The interior spaces are arranged on three levels: a raised basement, the main floor, and a partial second floor. The entry which is midway between the basement and main-floor levels, is actually a landing of the open stair constructed of steel and laminated wood. The basement was designed to provide a two-car garage, furnace room, recreation room, study/guest room, bath and darkroom. The top floor contains bedrooms and bath for two sons.

The main floor of the house has a spaciousness not readily apparent from the exterior. The living room is a large one, with a ceiling of suspended cedar paneling that follows the slope of the roof to a maximum height of 14 feet. A window wall and balcony open the space fully to the view. A low-ceilinged dining space is separated from the living area by a freestanding fireplace, yet the rooms are strongly tied together by a floor of red quarry tile—which covers all the main floor except for the carpeted master bedroom. A compact kitchen, with an adjoining laundry room, is placed between the dining area and the entrance stairs for convenience to all parts of the house.

MEILLEUR RESIDENCE, Bellevue, Washington. Owners: *Mr. and Mrs. Peter Meilleur.* Mechanical engineer: *Richard Stern.* Landscape architects: *Richard Haag Associates.* Contractor: *Pacific Northwest Construction Co.*

Hugh N. Stratford photos

BALCONY LEVEL
455 SQ. FT.

B.R. 2
11x13

BATH

B.R. 3
10x10

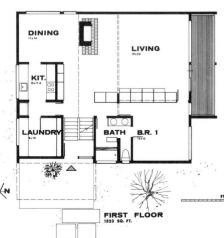

DINING
11x14

LIVING
19x23

KIT.
8x11·6

LAUNDRY
8x10

BATH

B.R. 1
12x13

FIRST FLOOR
1323 SQ. FT.

The openness of the living-dining and entrance areas of the house is further extended by using a balcony as hallway to the upper-level bedrooms (photo, near right). The structure of the house is wood frame, surfaced with oil-stained red cedar on the exterior, painted plasterboard on the interiors. Aluminum sash is used throughout. Furnace and water heater are both gas fired. The master bath is compartmented, and its counter is tiled in Venetian glass.

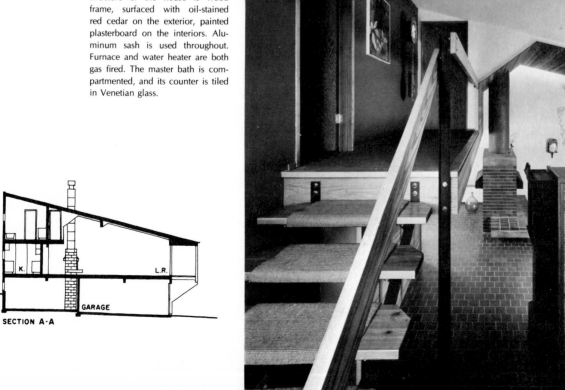

Christian Staub photos

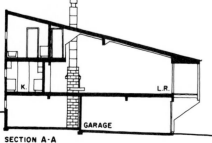

SECTION A-A

Norman Jaffe
Sagaponac, New York
1971

The strong, contained forms of this beach house reflect a remarkable arrangement of interior spaces within— many levels to effectively zone the house into activity areas, and windows unusually placed to provide panoramic, and sometimes unexpected views. The basic shape of the house is consciously geared to its site. Architect Jaffe comments that, "the site is a dune, a capricious cross section of sand meeting water, subject to the winds and the shifting of the tides. The shape of the dune is permissive, demanding a structure with a stance of its own: the 'feet' of the house are column extensions of wooden piles driven to below sea level on the land side of the dune; the columns continue up to become a roof returning to overhang the openings facing the ocean; the roof on the land side turns downward echoing the sliding return of the dune."

All this is sheathed—roof and walls—in cedar shakes, which helps to both unify and dramatize the sculptural qualities of the protrusions and insets of the design. To anchor the house solidly to its site, rough-hewn granite is used as a podium, extended to form an entrance court and retaining wall for the living room terrace at the top of the dune (see photos at left and below).

The lowest of the levels which zone the house contains the entry and childrens' rooms. The latter have a separate entrance and little terrace on the east facade of the house (photo bottom left). A free-standing stair leads up one-half level to an area for guests, with bedroom, studio and bath. Spiraling above this are the living areas (living room, dining room, kitchen and gallery), each of which are a few steps above the other. The top level or zone contains the master bedroom, studio, master bath, and a deck which cantilevers over the crest of the dune (photos below).

Very out-of-the-ordinary windows are used to give daylight and good views to this rising succession of spaces. At the front of the house a large window is notched into the facade to give a long down-slope vista from the main stair, and another window/skylight is set into front wall and roof to give sky views and light to both a guest room (photo below center) and to the higher-level gallery leading to the master bedroom floor (see section overleaf). Extra light is given to the gallery by a long skylight over the living room (see photo below). The main living rooms have wide banks of sliding glass walls facing the ocean, as does the master bedroom. The latter also has a little window to the east for view and morning sun.

The combination of the unusually placed and sized windows, the projections of the various cantilevers, and the skin-like "wrapping" of cedar shakes give the relatively small house an arresting, and eye-deceiving sense of monumental scale without compromise to its overall sense of warmth and comfort.

PERLBINDER RESIDENCE, Sagaponac, New York. Owners: *Mr. and Mrs. Stephen Perlbinder.* Architect: *Norman Jaffe.* Structural engineer: *James Romeo.* Contractor: *Stephen Perlbinder.*

The small photos above show the effect from inside the house of some of the unorthodox windows. At left is a little room on the guest level which is roofed by a window skylight. The master bedroom (above) has both views and a sense of seclusion.

A

B

C

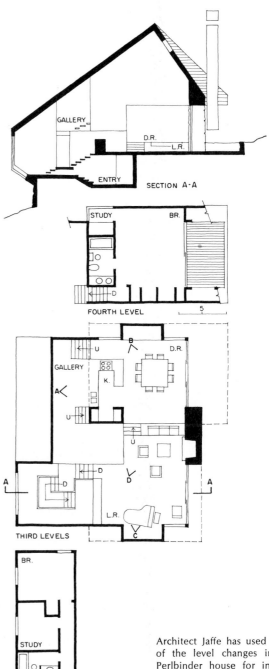

SECTION A·A

FOURTH LEVEL

THIRD LEVELS

SECOND LEVEL

FIRST LEVEL

Architect Jaffe has used some of the level changes in the Perlbinder house for innovative purposes. The step-up to the dining area, for example, is used to frame a built-in sofa, and the floor of the gallery level forms a generous sink-counter for the kitchen. The gallery also extends as a sitting balcony overlooking the living and stair areas.

As on the exterior, a single material helps weld all the levels together: all of the walls, ceilings, cabinets and built-in furniture are Douglas fir, and the floors are either of the same material or of Pennsylvania slate.

D

Jefferson Riley
Guilford
Connecticut
1978

For this evergreen, stone-chocked New England site, architect Jefferson Riley designed his own house using traditional materials and time-honored building techniques. It is a tall house (four stories including basement) and it rises in a complex profile of setback and projection in each elevation. Dormers protrude from the sleepy pitched roof, adding to this sense of complication, and all exterior surfaces are richly mottled with shadow.

The south-facing gable end of the house is opened generously to the sun. The greenhouse below and the varied openings above fill the tall space behind with natural light and warmth. Surplus solar heat collected in the greenhouse is circulated along the insulated foundation wall and stored for radiation at night. The second and third floor bedrooms are set back from the exterior wall but open through windows to the tall space, thus taking advantage of light and view without additional heat loss. Supplementary heating is provided by wood stoves in the kitchen and living room. These stoves vent through the roof and the tall flues accent the verticality of the design.

The volumetric liveliness of the Riley house comes from the interplay of intimate spaces with the unexpectedly tall central space and additional fun is provided by unlooked-for details for double-hung windows on interior walls or a panelled wood door leading to the greenhouse.

Of his non-mainstream approach to design Riley says: "The house with its long gable roof, its double-hung windows, its red-stained clapboards, its central chimney, its over-all bilateral symmetry offset by asymmetrical parts, makes numerous allusions to colonial houses indigenous to its New England context. Yet we did not reproduce these traits by rote, but found joy in assembling them into a unique composition with contemporary strivings of its own."

RILEY HOUSE, Guilford, Connecticut. Architect: *Jefferson Riley of Moore Grover Harper*. Contractor: *Essex Builders*.

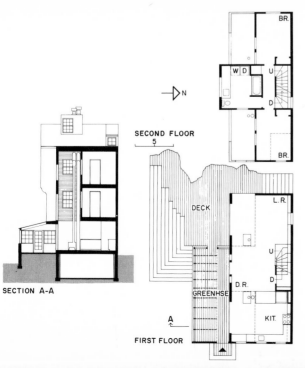

SECTION A-A

SECOND FLOOR

BR.

W D | U
D

BR.

DECK

L.R.

U
D

D.R.

GREENHSE.

KIT.

A

FIRST FLOOR

N

5

Graham Gund
Massachusetts
1979

Like any good New England house, this one on the Massachusetts coast is full of regional and historical imagery. But architect Graham Gund has freshly examined this imagery—creating a house that is in every detail appropriate to its site and the family that lives there.

The site is a small peninsula with ocean views in three directions. The problem was to take into account not just the sun and southern views, but also the persistent summer winds off Buzzards Bay. The solution, a three-part structure, surrounds and protects a courtyard which is central to the house not just physically but symbolically. The plan reflects the family's pattern of living: the owner's children and grandchildren visit in the summer. Thus, a winterized section (left, large photo) for the owners has a kitchen and dining room, a living room with large windows and a porch facing the view, and an upstairs master bedroom and den. A second section (right in photo) is for warm-weather use only, with its family spaces, four bedrooms, three "hide-a-way" lofts, all connected with outdoor walks, stair, and second-level boardwalk. The third section is garage and storage area, topped with a tower reached by ladder.

There are private outdoor spaces for both families (plan, overleaf), but the courtyard is the primary, shared living area—a stage for many family activities enlivened by changes in level, by freestanding, squared-off "archways" that create outdoor rooms and frame the view, and by subtle colors (white, beige, pale blue, pale salmon) on the clapboarded walls and gates. Around the outside, in the local vernacular, are simple weathered shingles.

Photos: © Steve Rosenthal

SHAPLEIGH RESIDENCE, Massachusetts. Owners: *Mr. and Mrs. Warren M. Shapleigh.* Architects: *Graham Gund Associates, Inc.—job captain: David Perry.* Structural engineer: *Souza & True.* Color consultant: *Tina Bebe.* Contractor: *Mishaum Construction Company.*

The interiors all have a sense of great shelter, and are detailed with great care. Yet, since the sections of the house are uniformly 16 feet deep, most rooms have a view not just of the courtyard but of the stunning coastline in three directions. At left is the kitchen in the main house; below left and opposite the living room of the main house; below right in the living room of the guest house. The plans show how the sections of the house create the sheltered courtyard, and show the organization of the court into private outdoor sections for both families, and into open and sunny, or sheltered and shaded, spaces. From both the road side and the beach side, changes in level and freestanding gateways create a sense of arrival. . . .

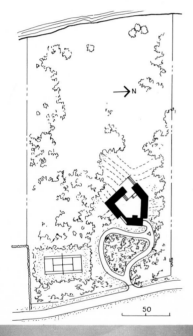

FIRST FLOOR 5 GARAGE SECOND FLOOR

Bill Maris photos

Gwathmey & Henderson

Purchase New York

1968

Excellent proof that a fresh, visually interesting building can be created within the framework of fairly stringent design codes is furnished by this handsome house. Local ordinances restricted building in the community to two-and-a-half stories in height, with a minimum of 35,000 cubic feet enclosed, and mandatory pitched roofs at not less than 6/12 slope. There were also minimum cost restrictions. Apart from the desire for a strong contemporary design, the owners' requirements were quite simple: living area, dining space, kitchen and powder room at grade level, three bedrooms and two baths above.

The white-stuccoed, terne-roofed geometric forms which evolved are probably remote from the designs the code-writers envisaged they were espousing, but following them to the letter has produced one of the most creatively significant houses of the year.

The site is a large, wooded one of 25 acres. The architects have placed the house in a private clearing within the woodland in a manner aimed at creating a series of "visual experiences". They describe it as follows: "having meandered up the winding drive, catching glimpses through the trees of the house, one arrives in a parking area. With the future addition of a garage and guest house (conceived of as a gate) the scale change from vehicular to pedestrian movement is made specific. From there, a variety of vistas, intensities and directions of light, and changes of shapes and dimensions, hopefully achieve the spatial richness and vitality we desire. Terminating the internal sequence is a complex configuration tying upper living space and stairhall to the anchoring fireplace: here one sees back across the clearing to the enveloping woodland."

Architects: Charles Gwathmey and Richard Henderson of Gwathmey & Henderson. *Location:* Purchase, New York. *Contractor:* Caramagna, Barbagallo & La Vito. *Landscape architects and interior designers:* Gwathmey & Henderson.

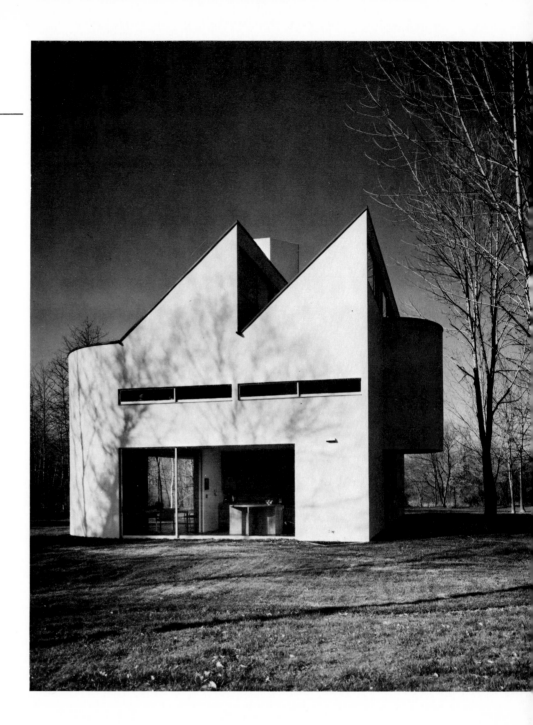

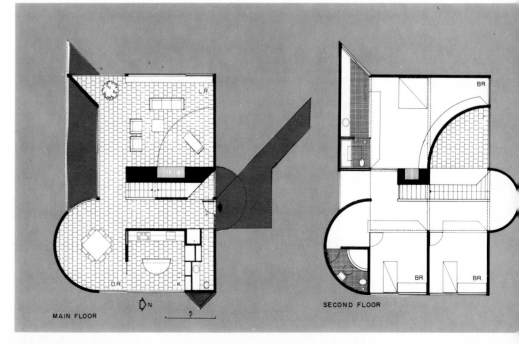

MAIN FLOOR   SECOND FLOOR

Charles Gwathmey and Richard Henderson have unified their strong architectural design in this house by planning the interiors and landscaping as well. Thus all, including the owners' harp in its special niche, has an unusual functional and visual compatibility.

As the architects stressed in their comments on the preceding page, room shapes and window placement have been studiedly varied to produce a constantly changing sequence of woodland views and lighting effects. Artificial lighting has been built-in to add yet other effects.

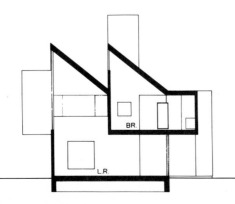

Barnstone & Aubry
Houston, Texas
1965

A steel and glass living-dining room, which seems almost to be suspended among the trees, is unquestionably the most dramatic feature of what is in any case an unusually interesting scheme. The enormous living pavilion consists of a 55-foot-by-30-foot steel truss resting on four 4-foot-by-4-foot brick columns. The architect said that the unusual shape of the steel framing was governed by engineering considerations, but this has the effect of enhancing the appearance of the structure and preventing it looking like an oversized glass box. Detailing and execution have been meticulously handled, showing how effectively steel can be used in domestic architecture.

Inside, the living room and dining room together from an impressive interior space. The glass is tinted so that sunlight is never accompanied by glare. Shades are provided for additional protection when required. The Mahers' collection of antique furniture has been used to great advantage in this eminently 20th century setting. The furniture has been placed in contemporary groupings, and great care has been taken not to over-furnish so that the effect of the space is in no way impaired.

The architect says that the house was conceived of in two masses, the front mass containing entry, bedrooms and all family spaces, while the back mass consists of the huge living room, with a parking space beneath.

Photos: Frank Lotz Miller

MAHER RESIDENCE, Houston, Texas. Owners: *Mr. and Mrs. John Maher.* Architect: *Howard Barnstone and Partner, Eugene Aubry.* Structural engineer: *R. George Cunningham.* Landscape architect: *Thomas Church.* Interior designer: Wells Design. Contractor: *Ivanhoe Construction Company.*

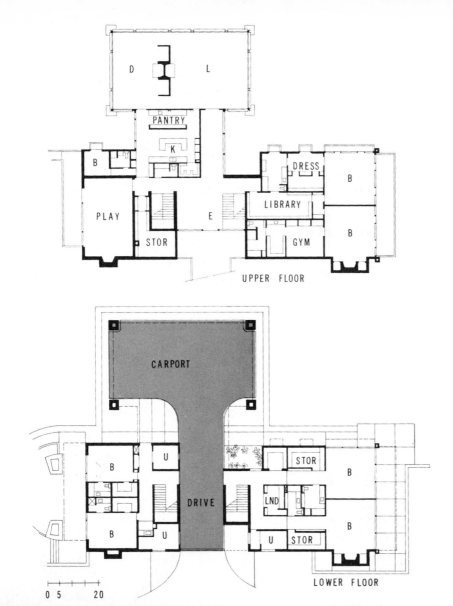

UPPER FLOOR

LOWER FLOOR

0 5   20

Although the living pavilion is the highlight of the Maher residence, the rest of the house is also very well planned and provides a great variety of unusual living areas. The master bedroom suite is particularly luxurious, consisting as it does of two large adjoining rooms, one with a spacious dressing room and the other with a private gymnasium attached. A library between the two bedrooms makes a conveninet place for quiet and study. Wherever possible balconies are provided overlooking the trees and a small bayou or creek. The children's entrance on the lower level gives convenient access to their bedrooms.

The mechanical system for a house of this size is important and presents certain problems. The architect describes how these were solved: ''the mechanical system includes five separate cooling systems interconnected by hot water heating and a common return through the shallow 'attic' between floors. The purpose of the separate systems is that the house be not vulnerable to total breakdown in the event of failure of a single compressor. With the common return, one of the systems may be inoperative, and the house would still be livable. Separated systems also provide a natural form of 'zone' control.''

Interior walls are gypsum board, plaster or wood paneling. Ceilings for the lower level are wood; for the rest of the house acoustic plaster is used.

Barton Myers
Toronto
Ontario
1977

There have been earlier attempts (few as successful) in Canada, the U.S. and elsewhere to blur the distinction between industrial and residential design vocabularies. Perhaps it was always a needless distinction, but it is still stimulating to see the steel columns, metal deck and the delicate tracery of open web joists transfer their precise elegance from factory to home so easily and persuasively. Inside the basic framework that these elements create is a secondary level of modification and texturing. It includes sculptured ductwork that traces powerful linear patterns throughout the house. It includes drop screens that temper the daylight at outside wall or skylight. And it also includes the entirely appropriate use of unexpected hardware and fixtures that are always within the residential designer's reach but seldom find their way into his specifications. It is a beautifully conceived house and even those whose cup of tea it is not will find much to linger over in its use of materials and its details.

The plan of the Wolf house is deceptively simple. It is a two-story, rectangular volume with a bite out of the center of one of its long sides—a bite which admits light and offers views from the normally "dead" waist section of such plans.

The house is lifted above the site to minimize the foundation problems that might otherwise have developed on 20 feet of new fill over a subterranean stream. The upper level contains bedrooms, baths, play area and study. Below, the principal spaces are arranged to take advantage of views to the park at the west. The closed side of the house, clad in aluminum siding, faces neighbors to the east.

In its rhythms, its textures and the handling of its details, the Wolf residence is beautifully organized and very skillfully executed.

WOLF HOUSE, Toronto, Ontario. Owners: *Lawrence and Mary Wolf.* Architect: *Barton Myers, formerly of A. J. Diamond & Barton Myers.* Structural engineers: *Read Jones Christoffersen, Ltd.* Foundations: *William Trow Associates, Ltd.* Mechanical engineers: *G. Granek Associates, Ltd.* Cost consultant: *A. J. Vermeulen, Inc.* Contractor: *Lawrence Wolf.*

SECOND FLOOR — BR. STUDY BATH BR. PLAY BR. BR. LAUN

FIRST FLOOR — L.R. DINING KIT. CARPORT MECH. 5

Photos: T. Kitajima of Y. Futagawa & Associates, except as noted

The owner's comment, in describing his vision of the house, is significant: "We saw the house as the ultimate new product, the mass market space and flexibility solution of the future."

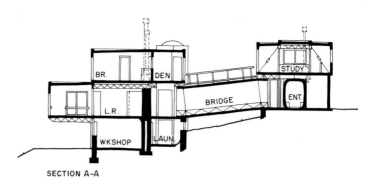

SECTION A-A

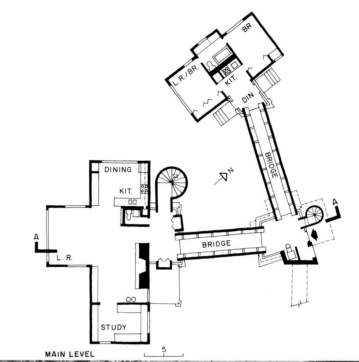

MAIN LEVEL

Johansen-Bhavnani
Connecticut
1978

The principal influence on this design was the site itself—a beautiful but sharply sloping hillside vexed by massive rock shelves and outcroppings that left only three small areas suitable for building. Using these spots as shoulders, Johansen developed a fragmented plan, piling up rock foundations for each of the three main elements of the plan, then cantilevering the house over these foundations to save as many root systems of close-in trees as possible.

Bringing the parts of the house together—and giving due visual importance to circulation in so decentralized a scheme—are tubes designed in what architect and owner smilingly call "a Budd Car esthetic." These wonderfully expressive elements are made structural by bar joists under the floor, and are finished in corrugated aluminum sheet that serves as a foil against the site—a site on which Nature appears to have pulled out all her stops. Where tube and glass wall intersect, a neoprene gasket is introduced to create a seal and water shields keep run-off along the corrugations from reaching the glass wall. Gaskets, shields, grommets and associated hardware are all stock industrial items. Inside (see photos next pages) the tubes are finished, insulated, and fitted with concealed lighting.

The house is framed in a combination of light steel and wood stud and clad in an asbestos-cement panel with a factory finish used here in several contrasting colors.

The interiors of the main spaces are dressed in gypsum board, slate, field stone and wood plank, materials that return us to the realm of the familiar. More than anything else, perhaps, it is this conjunction of the familiar with the unfamiliar that gives this house its richness, its strength, its fun and, above all, its special claim on the attention of the profession.

PRIVATE RESIDENCE, Connecticut. Architects: *Johansen-Bhavnani.* Structural engineers: *Besier & Gibble.* Mechanical engineers: *Flack & Kurtz.* Contractor: *A. and L. Zavagnin.*

Photos: David Hirsch

The closed character of the tubes is in marked contrast to the rest of the house, which is opened almost everywhere to views of the site and the Connecticut countryside beyond. Double glazing is used in all major openings.

Richard Meier
Darien, Connecticut
1968

Forceful, direct expression of the plan organization and of the zoning of activities gives this house a freshly handsome, totally unstereotyped character. Thus, the dramatically handled interior spaces are, in projection, used to create an artfully stylized exterior. Design impact is produced by the simplest means, with no frills and a remarkable absence of most current architectural cliches.

Architect Meier states, with equal simplicity, "there is a straight-forward use of a wood bearing-wall and framing system for the enclosed half of the building, coordinated with a steel columnar structure for the open living spaces. This allows for a direct expression of the nature of living and service areas with respect to orientation, view and use. Glass is used extensively in the living areas, while a closed-wall expression is maintained by the use of vertical wood siding for private areas."

The house was designed for a family with two children, and located on a beautiful site of rocky, wooded, irregular terrain overlooking Long Island Sound. Rooms are disposed on three levels, with the "main" floor in the center. The entrance hall, living area and master bedroom suite are on this middle level (a slope in the land made possible outside exits on two levels). The top floor contains children's bedrooms, guest room and library-play area—which forms a balcony. The lower level is for dining, kitchen, laundry and domestic help. Both the living and the dining areas open directly to outdoor terraces, and the house is topped by an outdoor roof deck. Meier adds that "all the living spaces are interconnected vertically: the living area opening up to the library and down to the dining room. They constitute the open aspect of the house and focus upon the view of the water."

SMITH HOUSE, Darien, Connecticut. Owners: *Mr. and Mrs. Fred Smith.* Architect: *Richard Meier.* Engineer: *William Atlas.* Contractor: *Ernest Rau.*

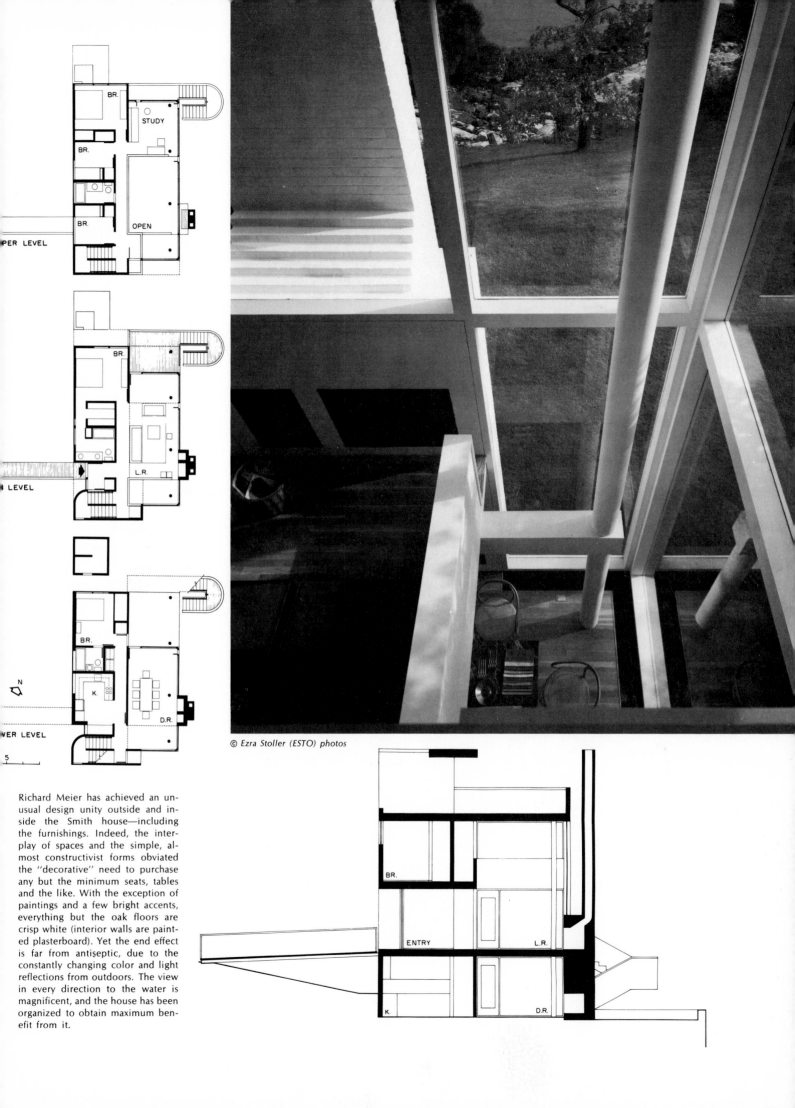

© *Ezra Stoller (ESTO) photos*

Richard Meier has achieved an unusual design unity outside and inside the Smith house—including the furnishings. Indeed, the interplay of spaces and the simple, almost constructivist forms obviated the "decorative" need to purchase any but the minimum seats, tables and the like. With the exception of paintings and a few bright accents, everything but the oak floors are crisp white (interior walls are painted plasterboard). Yet the end effect is far from antiseptic, due to the constantly changing color and light reflections from outdoors. The view in every direction to the water is magnificent, and the house has been organized to obtain maximum benefit from it.

"Don't worry—If you love it enough it will love you back."

"Do I have to live in a 'statement?' Can't I just have a home?"

INDEX

"One thing more—it still takes a heap o' livin', you know."